921
MYE
CPS—MORRILL SCHOOL ☑ W9-BBN-012

Bad boy.

34880030036516

813.54
~~921~~
MYE

Myers, Walter Dean,
   1937-

Bad boy.

C.1 Q

34880030036516

$22.95

DATE			

CPS—MORRILL SCHOOL
CHICAGO PUBLIC SCHOOLS
6011 S ROCKWELL STREET
CHICAGO, IL 60629
03/13/2006

BAKER & TAYLOR

BAD BOY

*Also by Walter Dean Myers
in Large Print:*

The Dream Bearer
Shooter
Monster

BAD BOY

a memoir

Walter Dean Myers

Thorndike Press • Waterville, Maine

421
mue
c.1u
2004
22.45

Recommended for Young Adult Readers.

Copyright © 2001 by Walter Dean Myers

All rights reserved.

Published in 2005 by arrangement with HarperCollins
Children's Books, a division of HarperCollins Publishers Inc.

Thorndike Press® Large Print The Literacy Bridge.

The tree indicium is a trademark of Thorndike Press.

The text of this Large Print edition is unabridged.
Other aspects of the book may vary from the original edition.

Set in 16 pt. Plantin by Ramona Watson.

Printed in the United States on permanent paper.

Library of Congress Cataloging-in-Publication Data

Myers, Walter Dean, 1937–
    Bad boy : a memoir / by Walter Dean Myers. —
Large print ed.
      p. cm.
    ISBN 0-7862-7537-5 (lg. print : hc : alk. paper)
    1. Myers, Walter Dean, 1937– — Childhood and youth —
Juvenile literature. 2. Authors, American — 20th century
— Biography — Juvenile literature. 3. African American
authors — Biography — Juvenile literature. 4. Children's
stories — Authorship — Juvenile literature. 5. Large type
books. I. Title.
PS3563.Y48Z47 2005
813′.54—dc22   2005000114

For Karen, Michael, and Christopher

Contents

Roots

Each of us is born with a history already in place. There are physical aspects that make us brown-eyed or blue-eyed, that make us tall or not so tall, or give us curly or straight hair. Our parents might be rich or poor. We could be born in a crowded, bustling city or in a rural area. While we live our own individual lives, what has gone before us, our history, always has some effect on us. In thinking about what influenced my own life, I began by considering the events and people who came before me. I learned about most of the people who had some effect on my life through family stories, census records, old photographs, and, in the case of Lucas D. Dennis, the records of the Works Progress Administration at the University of West Virginia.

The Works Progress Administration was a government program formed to create jobs during the Depression years. It did this by starting a number of projects, including state histories. Among the notes of

9

the interviewers putting together a history of West Virginia, I came across this entry.

Life of a Slave

Lucas D. Dennis was one of the one hundred and fifty slaves that Steve Dandridge owned before the Civil War. This slave is ninety-four years old. He was born in Jefferson County. His mind is very bright, he still has two of his own teeth, his hair is gray and [he] wears a heavy beard which is also gray.

After the Civil War he came to Harpers Ferry and built himself a house, which is on one of the camping grounds used during the war. This house is on Filmore Ave. and the corner of a lane leading to where many soldiers were buried and later taken up and carried to their burial ground in Winchester.

He lives with his wife, she is eighty-four. He saw John Brown and remembers well the day he was hanged.

Lucas D. Dennis was my great-great-uncle. Prior to the Civil War, when West Virginia was still part of the state of Virginia, these ancestors of mine were slaves on a plantation called The Bower, in Leetown, Virginia. The 1870 census still listed Lucas D. Dennis as living on the plantation, but I knew, from family stories, that he did indeed move to Harpers Ferry and that part of the Dennis family moved to Martinsburg, West Virginia, less than ten miles from The Bower. At the time of the interview with Lucas D. Dennis, the Dennis family in Martinsburg had merged with the Green family. One of the women of the Green family, Mary Dolly Green, later became my mother.

I have no memory of Mary Dolly Green. I know that she gave birth to me on a Thursday, the twelfth of August, 1937. I have been told that she was tall, with a fair complexion. Mary had five children: Gertrude, Ethel, George, me, and Imogene. Shortly after the birth of my sister Imogene my mother died, leaving my father, George Myers, with seven children, two of them, Geraldine and Viola, from a previous marriage. When I imagine my mother, I think of an attractive young woman with the same wide smile as my sisters'. I wish I could have known her. However, today, when I think of "mother," I think of another woman, my father's first wife, Florence Dean.

Florence Dean's mother emigrated from Germany in the late 1800s. A cook by profession, Mary Gearhart settled outside Chambersburg, Pennsylvania, in New Franklin, Pennsylvania. There she met and married a Native American by the name of Brown. The couple had one daughter, Florence. Mary Gearhart, a small, pleasant woman, worked at a number of restaurants before finding a job in a German hotel in Martinsburg, West Virginia.

When Florence was old enough to work, she also came to Martinsburg. It was while working at the hotel that she met a young black man, George Myers. The two young people began to see each other socially and were married when Florence was seventeen. From this marriage came two children, Geraldine and Viola. Unfortunately, the marriage ended in divorce, and Florence returned to Pennsylvania. The fact that Florence had married a black man did not sit well with her German relatives, and she was made to feel unwelcome. She decided to move to Baltimore, Maryland, where she met Herbert Dean.

Herbert Dean lived in Baltimore with his father, stepmother, two sisters, Nancy and Hazel, and his brother, Leroy. His father, William Dean, was a tall, handsome, and opinionated man who had little use for formal education aside from reading the Bible, and even less use for women. He ran a small hauling business in Baltimore that consisted of several wagons and teams of horses. He expected his sons to enter the business when they were of age. When trucks began to replace horses and wagons, he scoffed at the idea, labeling the trucks as a mere fad that would never last. Even as his business declined, he stubbornly stuck to his beliefs. By the time he was nine, Herbert Dean was already working, pulling a wagon through the streets of the city, collecting scraps of wood, cutting it for kindling, and selling it door to door to light the fires in the old coal stoves that most people had at the time. Herbert had left school after the third grade, realizing that he was needed to help support the family.

By the time Herbert reached manhood, his father's hauling business was no more than a way of making a few dollars on occasion, and when William Dean still declined to invest in trucks, both of the boys struck out on their own. Leroy decided to remain in the Baltimore area, and Herbert decided to try his luck in New York City. Herbert had met a woman who interested him. She had been married previously and had two children, but now she was single and still quite attractive. The woman, Florence, was white, and that posed a problem in Baltimore. Perhaps, Herbert thought, it would be less of a problem in New York.

Herbert and Florence married and moved to Harlem. Herbert first found work with a moving company owned by the gangster Dutch Schultz. Each morning, men would line up on the street corners, and the Schultz trucks would pick up as many men as they needed that day. When Schultz was not hiring, there were occasional jobs to be had at the docks, loading and unloading ships. Eventually, Herbert found a permanent job as a janitor with the United States Radium Corporation in downtown New York.

As a young couple Herbert and Florence made the Harlem party scene. When Herbert's boyhood friend Chick Webb came to New York, he introduced Herbert to some of his show-business pals such as Bill Robinson and Fats Waller. Herbert even entertained the idea of getting into music and bought a slide trombone at a pawnshop. Florence hated the trombone, disliked jazz, and wanted to be reunited with her daughters, who were

14

still living in Martinsburg with their father.

Herbert agreed to bring Florence's two daughters, Geraldine and Viola, to New York and drove down to Martinsburg in the black Ford he had bought. It was during this visit that he met George Myers, Florence's first husband, her two daughters, and George's children by Mary Myers.

The girls were brought to Harlem, and several months later it was decided that Herbert and Florence would also take the youngest boy, Walter Milton Myers.

Harlem

Harlem is the first place called "home" that I can remember. It was a magical place, alive with music that spilled onto the busy streets from tenement windows and full of colors and smells that filled my senses and made my heart beat faster. The earliest memory I have is of a woman who picked me up on Sunday mornings to take me to Sunday school. She would have five to ten children with her when she rang our bell on 126th Street, and we would go through the streets holding hands and singing "Jesus Loves Me" on our way to Abyssinian Baptist. I remember being comforted by the fact that Jesus, whom I didn't even know, thought so much of me. After church we would be brought home, again holding hands and singing our way through the streets of Harlem.

What life was about for me in those early years was being with the woman I was learning to call Mama. When Florence Dean was home, I would follow her from

16

room to room as she cleaned, talking about anything that came to mind, knowing that she would always listen. Any house in which she lived was kept spotless. Mama had a time to sweep the floors and a time to mop them. There was a time to wash clothes and a time to iron them, fold them, and put them away. Each holiday meant taking all the dishes down from the shelves, even the ones we never used, and carefully washing and drying them, as well as the windows of the dish cabinet.

Mama didn't work outside the house when I first arrived in New York, but that changed from time to time. I remember that when I was four, a woman in the building was taken on as my caretaker during the days when Mama worked. Mama did what she called "day's work," meaning that she cleaned other people's apartments and was paid by the day. The woman who took care of me gave that chore to her children, who delighted in torturing me by hiding in the closet and making believe they were ghosts. I was a bawler, screaming in fear at all the appropriate moments, which delighted them. I learned how mindlessly cruel some children could be.

We were far away from credit cards in

those days, and the equivalent was an account at the corner grocery. Mama, who was determined that I should never be hungry, arranged with the grocer to give me food if I was hungry and to put it on her account. What I actually did when I had the chance was buy penny squares of chocolate. Soon every kid on the block knew that I could get "free" chocolates. One weekend both the grocer and I got a good talking-to, and my account came to a crashing end.

What I loved most about Harlem, though, was the music. There were radios everywhere, and little girls jumped double Dutch to Duke Ellington, Cab Calloway, and Glenn Miller. My sisters, Gerry and Viola, danced with me in the house, but the girls in the street wouldn't dance with me, so I danced by myself. I had taught myself a little dance that I called "the boogie." My dancing was amusing enough for people to throw pennies to me when I danced. When I had enough pennies, I would scoop them up and run to the grocer's to buy my favorite colored icy pops. I could keep this up for hours and loved it until one day I had a stomachache and went home crying. When Mama got home from work, she put me on the toilet and sat on the edge of the bathtub to comfort me. Within minutes I was being snatched up and rushed to Knickerbocker Hospital. Mama had reasoned that the red liquid passing through my intestines had to be blood. At the hospital the doctors were equally alarmed until a few tests confirmed that I had consumed so many icy pops that the food coloring was going straight through. It was clear I needed more supervision during the day, and Mama found another baby-sitter, who took care of a number of children.

This woman had playground apparatus in her backyard, which I liked a lot. I was told not to play on the climbing bars, but I tried them anyway. Getting to the top was easy enough and not nearly as exciting as falling off, headfirst, onto the cement below. I've always had a big head, and I must have looked a sight that night, with bandages covering half my face, when Mama picked me up. She decided to stay home to take care of me for a while.

My two sisters were already in their teens and had the job of being young ladies. I was the baby of the family and the only boy and got most of the attention, which I enjoyed. I claimed Mama for my own and was jealous of any attention she paid to her daughters. When Gerry received a fancy watch as a present, I was annoyed. Gerry hadn't changed, and so I thought it was the watch that made her special.

"Can I have a nickel?" I asked Mama. A week had passed since Gerry had received the watch, and Mama, her forehead dripping sweat, was doing the wash in a tub of scalding water, pushing the sheets down into the hot liquid with a stick. Mama shook her head.

"Can I have a nickel?" I asked again, wanting her to stop the washing and perhaps take me to the corner store for an icy pop.

"Later, Walter," she said. "I'm busy now. Go play."

"I'll break Gerry's watch," I said.

"Boy, go into the living room and play!" she said, sternly.

The watch didn't break right away. I hit it with my shoe, and nothing happened. Then I hit it with my father's shoe, and it still didn't break. Then I hit it with both shoes as hard as I could until I saw a crack in the curved crystal. This I took proudly to Mama.

A spanking is a spanking is a spanking. Mama was strong enough to hold me by the corner of my shirt at the shoulder and lift me so that I could not get a firm footing on the ground. Then, still sweating from her efforts at washing the sheets, she laced into me with a folded belt that, from that time on, became "the strap." Of course, she could have prevented the watch from being broken if she had only believed me when I told her that I was going to break it. Instead she covered my legs and hands with welts with the strap. When Gerry came home from work, she wasn't pleased, either.

I needed discipline, but my adoptive father, Herbert Dean, hated to see me crying. So the next time Mama worked outside the house, I was sent to my aunt Nancy, my father's sister, who lived in downtown New York.

Division Street on New York's Lower East Side was as wonderful to me as Harlem. There were few black people in the area, but at my age, which was probably five, I was not really aware of racial differences. What was on Division Street was Aunt Nancy, her husband, whom we all called Mr. Harrison, the bakery she operated, pushcarts, a matzoh factory, and Jewish boys. Mama would take me to Aunt Nancy's on a Sunday night and pick up the following Friday.

Aunt Nancy was as fat as she was tall. She was the biggest woman I had ever seen in my life and exactly the same color brown as my father. I liked her because she was a friendly woman, but I absolutely hated the idea that she would take naps in the middle of the day. What's more, she would insist that I take naps with her, which I thought was a terrible thing to do. I never wanted to go to sleep, not even at night when it was dark. Certainly I didn't want to go to sleep in the middle of the day. Still, every afternoon she would come upstairs from the bakery and head for the bed.

In Aunt Nancy's living room was a cast-iron alligator ashtray that was nearly as tall as I was. It had glass eyes and hard cast-iron scales down its back. More than once I thought I saw one of its glass eyes look in my direction. It was not my favorite object.

Aunt Nancy spent most of the day working in the bakery. In the afternoons I was allowed to play in front of the store. That's where I met the boys who told me we could beat up some of the Jewish boys.

The Jewish boys always came downstairs with their mothers. They wore their hair long on the side and sometimes wore shirts that seemed too big. If you hit them, they wouldn't hit back but would run to their mothers. I followed the example of some of the bigger boys and hit the ones who wouldn't hit back. The problem was, of course, that if you chased them around the corner, where their mothers couldn't see them, they would fight back. After a while a Jewish boy would stand near the corner, hoping that one of us would make the mistake of chasing him to a position where he could send his fist into an unsuspecting nose. If the men who worked in the matzoh factory saw us, they sometimes would separate us and give everyone hot baked matzohs. Wonderful.

Mama didn't always have to work outside the house. The greatest time I ever spent in my life was when she was home. During the day we would walk down the south side of 125th Street to the Smilen Brothers produce store or to Blumstein's, the largest store on 125th Street. The street was always busy, and black and white shoppers stopped in the shoe stores or bought charlotte russes to eat as they walked. We would walk east and then return on the north side of the street. The north side of the street had Herbert's Diamonds, a large jewelry store, and the better theaters. First we would stop at the RKO Alhambra to see what was playing, then the Loew's. Sometimes Mama would stop and look at the pictures outside the Apollo Theater, and sometimes, for a special treat, we would stop in the penny arcade. On rare occasions we would go all the way over to the East Side to the market stalls under the elevated railroad tracks.

If we didn't go out, we would listen to her soap operas on the radio. *Helen Trent* was her favorite. Mama also liked to read *True Romance* magazines and would let me sit on her lap as she read aloud.

The sound of Mama's voice in our sun-drenched Harlem kitchen was like a special kind of music, meant for only me. It was almost a secret language, one that only the two of us understood. I don't think she ever used that special voice with my sisters or my father. She was small, barely over five feet tall, and I was soon too big to sit on her lap. Then she would sit at the kitchen table, and I would sit on a chair with wooden arms and a fabric body that I loved and listen to the sound of her voice as she half read, half acted out the stories of lost loves and sudden passions.

I think she liked talking to me. She could tell me things she wouldn't tell other people. Once she told me that she liked to yodel and that she had done so as a child. She yodeled for me, and I thought it was marvelous. When I told my father, he laughed, and she wouldn't yodel for him. Sometimes she would ask me simple questions, like what did I think the weather would be the next day, and stop whatever she was doing and wait for an answer. I would have the words in my head and would try to get them out as quickly as I could, putting them in as good an order as I could.

"Why don't you just marry Mama?" my sister Viola complained. "You always have something to say to her."

I asked Mama about that later, and she said no, she already had a husband, Herbert.

Years later, when I had learned to use words better, I lost my ability to speak so freely with Mama.

I didn't want to learn to read so much as I wanted to be like Mama. I liked words and talking, and I wanted to be able to look at the magazines and tell her the stories as she did for me. I told her that I wanted to do this, and she rearranged our chairs so we were sitting side by side in the kitchen, with her pointing out the words as she read them. Slowly, with Mama's help, I learned to read. Before long I could read well enough to read to Mama as she did the housework. What we had to read were Mama's *True Romance* magazines and a few Classic comics. I didn't understand much of what I was reading, but I was on my way.

Let's Hear It for the First Grade!

When I first started school, I could read on a second-grade level, and it was suggested that I be put into that grade. I was as big as most second graders, too. My first-grade teacher, Mrs. Dworkin, said that it was a very bad idea.

"He can read on the second-grade level, but he can't speak well enough to be in the second grade."

I didn't know what she meant by that because I thought I spoke perfectly well. But I liked Mrs. Dworkin. She was a hugger, and whenever you did something good in her class, it ended up with her pulling you close and telling you just how good you were. I was in no hurry to leave her class.

We used a thick white paste to glue leaves and picture cutouts onto heavy construction paper. My only trouble in the first grade came when I accidentally dumped a jar of the paste onto my lap. A boy laughed, and I took some of the paste from my lap and put it on his. Mrs. Dworkin made me stand in a corner for almost an hour. Despite the "accident," I loved P.S. 125, and I loved school. It was a place where I could meet a lot of other kids my age, play games, and listen to the stories that Mrs. Dworkin would read to us. It wasn't until I reached the second grade that I realized that I had a speech problem.

"Dabba! Dabba! Dabba!" Manuel Bonilla taunted me, standing inches from my face and mimicking my poor speech as the rest of the class watched. "Dabba! Dabba! Dabba!"

Manuel stopped the "dabba-dabba-dabba" when I hit him in the face. When Mrs. Bower, our second-grade teacher, came into the room, the class was standing around Manuel, who lay still on the floor.

"Is he dead?" someone asked.

Of course Manuel wasn't anywhere near dead, but that didn't stop Mrs. Bower from sending me directly to the principal's office. Again.

Actually, I liked the principal's office. It was interesting to see the teachers come and go, talking about what they would have for lunch or what they had done the night before just as if they were normal people. I liked Mrs. Flynn, the principal, too. She was a tall, elegant woman who had a way of talking to pupils that made you feel good about yourself even if you were being punished.

My punishment, on this occasion, was to write five hundred times, "I will never, never hit any student in Public School 125."

Public School 125 on LaSalle Street had once been a police station. There were rumors of cells in the basement where the souls of dead prisoners, prisoners who had died in jail, howled all night. Being put down there would have been bad, and writing anything was much easier. What jail meant to me at the time was that you had to get some money together to get out. My father's brother, Leroy, called Lee, was in jail, and my father was constantly getting letters from lawyers asking for money for Uncle Lee's "case." I discovered that Uncle Lee had been in jail longer than I had been alive.

The one truly bad thing about being punished in the principal's office was that whenever Mrs. Bower was upset, she would stop teaching and read to us. She was in the middle of reading *Little House in the Big Woods*, and I was going to miss her reading because I was in the principal's office. I imagined Laura in the small cabin, and all kinds of bears and creepy things just feet from the front door, waiting to get in. Mrs. Bower had shown us a picture of Indians. They were half naked, dark, and scowling. All the images of Indians I had seen were negative. I never thought of Mama as an Indian, but I did worry about her father.

"Go to your class and ask for your homework assignment," Mrs. Flynn said. "You have to do your homework plus the five hundred times."

I went to class just before school was let out.

"Mrs. Bower said you were terrible," a boy informed me.

I didn't think I was terrible and gave him a good kick under the desk to emphasize the point.

At home, Mama asked me how school had been, and I told her it had been just fine.

The first thing I did was to write all the numbers down, from one to five hundred, in my notebook. I didn't believe how many pages it was going to take. Then I took a ruler and made a straight line down the left-hand side of each page. That straight line was going to be my "I" for each of the five hundred times. But when I wrote out the first "I will never, never . . ." I learned that I couldn't fit the sentence on one line. Life was not fair.

We had moved from 126th Street. Morningside Avenue, where our new apartment was located, was wide and beautiful. There were apartments on one side of the avenue and Morningside Park on the other. The park, I would learn later, was the western edge of Harlem. On the far side of the park were the Columbia University complex, Grant's Tomb, and Riverside Church, all places I would come to know over the following years. The building we lived in was a five-floor walkup — we lived on the fourth floor. At the top of each landing there was a gaslight fixture that was no longer being used now that the building was wired for electricity. The entrance hall was wide, with a tile floor. The first stairway consisted of about nine steps, a sharp turn, and then seven more steps to the landing of the second floor. When you were being chased, that turn always gave you an extra second to escape.

We lived between 121st and 122nd Streets, just three blocks from 125th

Street, Harlem's main thoroughfare. On the corner at 122nd Street was the Church of the Master, a fairly large Presbyterian church in which I would spend much of my early life. The church had a great old organ, with pipes that went from behind the organ to a point high overhead. The building next to the main part of the church had a gym and a stage. The ceiling in the gym was low, and you could tell which kid had learned to play basketball there by his flat jump shot.

My own apartment was, I believe, originally designed as a one-bedroom flat with a dining room, kitchen, living room, and nursery. Five of us moved into apartment 4S, and Mama was thrilled with the spaciousness of the arrangements. As many as ten or eleven people lived in some of the apartments, but most had only four to six. The apartments weren't designed for that many, but that was what Harlem was about, working people doing the best they could.

Second grade was most notable in my mind for the adventures of Laura, but we also had World War II. The kids all brought newspapers to school and, once a month, cans of food. My father was drafted into the Navy, and Mama and my sisters all got jobs in the garment industry. It was decided that I was old enough not to have a baby-sitter after school, and I was given my own house key.

"You're a big boy now," Mama said. "Make sure you lock the doors when you go out, and be sure to turn off the lights."

I was a big boy. At age eight I was bigger than most of my classmates and nearly as tall as Mama, who stood barely over five feet. In Bible school, which I attended summers at the Church of the Master, I had learned to weave a lanyard out of plastic strips. There was a clip at the end of the lanyard, and onto this I hooked the key ring. Almost all the kids in the neighborhood with working parents had their keys around their necks on either strings or plastic key chains made in Bible school.

Having my own house key was absolutely magnificent for two reasons. The first had to do with the grown-up feeling I got by unlocking and locking the door. The second reason had to do with Mrs. Dodson, the Wicked Witch of West Harlem. This woman worked very hard to ruin my life.

"Mrs. Dean, you shouldn't let that boy play with guns," she had announced the year before.

She had seen me chasing a friend down 121st Street, my Lone Ranger cap pistol blazing, and cornering him in front of 72 Morningside Avenue (the home of the Wicked Witch of West Harlem) before he could recock his Red Ryder carbine.

Mama considered Mrs. Dodson an educated Negro and someone to whom she should listen. My cap pistol was taken from me and, despite my tears, put out with the garbage. The next thing upon which Mrs. Dodson cast her evil eye was comic books.

"They're a road map to the jailhouse," she said.

I was told I could no longer bring comic books into the house. The Wicked Witch said that one day I would thank her for saving me. She didn't know me very well, and obviously she did not know about my next-door neighbor, Ralph "Roughie" Williams.

Roughie had more comic books than anyone else in the whole world. He was three years older than me, and we rarely spoke. But once a month he discarded a small stack of comic books, sometimes as many as fifteen and at times even twice that number. There they would be, sitting in a neat pile outside his door, waiting for the super to pick them up and take them down to the basement. As soon as I got the house keys, I knew that I had found a way to get those comics into the house. I took them in immediately if Mama wasn't home. If Mama was home, I would take the comics down to the first floor and hide them far underneath the stairs. Then, when Mama was safely off to work, I would sneak down and get them. Unlike Roughie, I saved my comics. Once I heard Mama tell a neighbor that I didn't read comics, but I knew I had close to two hundred tucked safely away under my bed.

I read well and I knew it, despite the fact that I never got the best marks in the class in reading. It seemed that whenever I got a C or a D in conduct, which was usual, it would drag down all my other marks as well. What I read away from school was comic books, as many as Roughie could afford.

The idea that the comics were forbidden added to their appeal. They could also be reread and traded, and I was soon known as the comic-book king of my set. The radio serials were like an extension of the comics, and Mama liked to listen to them with me.

In school I had started speech therapy.

Once a week a speech specialist would come to the school and work with the students who had speech problems, and I was considered one of those who had problems. The therapist kept trying to get me to pronounce my words clearly, but apparently I did not. The trouble was that to me, the words seemed clear. I found it frustrating when a teacher would ask me to repeat a phrase over and over, or when a teacher said that I did not know a word because I did not pronounce it correctly. There were things I was good at in school, such as reading and spelling, but it seemed to me that my speech somehow became more important than anything else. I would become very angry if kids laughed at my speech, or even if I thought they were laughing. My first instinct would be to yell at them, quickly followed by punching them.

Near the end of the year in the third grade, I slapped a kid, and my teacher, Mrs. Zeiss, slapped me. She slapped me at least once a day for the next week of schooldays until Dorothy Dodson (the daughter of the Wicked Witch) told her mother, who told my mother, who went to the school and told the teacher never to hit me again. Mrs. Zeiss didn't hit me again, but she failed me in reading, math, conduct, and everything else except gym and attendance. My report card was a mess of brightly colored red marks and circled grades. I even received a C in reading.

The one sure thing that would produce a beating in my house was a report card with a red mark in conduct. The idea that the teacher didn't like me did not count as far as conduct was concerned. I was beaten that night and told that over the summer I would have to relearn all the lessons in which I had done poorly. Mama, the one doing the beating, was really mad and threatened even more punishment. I didn't mind her threats because she never stayed mad. And, as my sister Gerry pointed out, I had been promoted to the fourth grade.

Arithmetic Summer

My sister Viola was married to a soldier, Frank Law, in 1944, and had a baby, Frank Stephen Law, in April 1945. When I brought home my report card at the end of the third grade, with all the bad marks circled in red, Mama was very upset. Frank, a graduate from a black college and a commercial artist, volunteered to help me with arithmetic, in which I had received my lowest mark. As I remember it, my arithmetic was as good as anyone's in the class, if not better, but the teacher had hated me and reminded me of that when she filled out my report card.

At first I was threatened with not being allowed to go to Bible school, which I loved, but eventually an arrangement was worked out. I would come directly home from Bible school and spend two hours working on math problems with Frank.

Frank's idea of arithmetic was rote learning. Every day I was given one hundred oral problems to solve. One miss meant that I would have to do another hundred. If he gave me a problem such as nine times seven, I would have to say "sixty-three" at once. "Uh, sixty-three" was considered a wrong answer. So was "Sixty, uh, three." I learned to hate arithmetic.

With Viola married and Gerry grown, I found myself sleeping on the couch in the living room. From where I lay, I could look out the window across Morningside Avenue all the way to the red light on top of Riverside Church. For some reason that red light was always a source of comfort to me, and many nights I fell asleep looking at it.

When school started in September, I was looking forward to it. Mama warned me to be on my best behavior this year, and I fully intended to do just that. I wanted to be good and do God's will, as I was being taught in church. I spent a lot of time in the church, and it meant a lot to me.

The pastor, Reverend James H. Robinson, was nice but strict. If he caught you throwing candy wrappers on the sidewalk, he would give you a whack with his open hand on the bottom hard enough to lift you off the ground. Or if you played Chinese handball against the wall during a funeral, he would send Mrs. Bellinger, one of the big-bosomed matrons, out to yell at you. No one could yell quite like Mrs. Bellinger.

School started in September, and I was going back to P.S. 125 on LaSalle Street in Harlem.

I met Eric Leonhardt in the fourth grade. He was blond and blue-eyed and lived over a bakery on Amsterdam Avenue in Morningside Heights. Eric's parents owned the bakery and worked in it as well. Mama had come to school for some kind of parents' meeting and sat next to his mother. His mother was German and spoke with an accent. She sat next to my Mama, and the two women talked, and Eric and I talked a little. I don't know how much German Mama spoke — I think she understood more than she could speak.

During the first week of the fourth grade Mrs. Parker, our teacher, made the two tallest boys, Eric and me, the cookie monitors. It was our job to take the cookie orders and then go down to the first floor to get the cookies and milk from the teacher who had charge of them for the day. The Sunshine bakery was in the neighborhood, and the cookies would still be warm and delicious. Sometimes Eric and I would open the cookies with cream in them and lick off part of the cream.

Mrs. Parker told me that she had heard all about me, and that if I did one thing wrong, she would make me sorry. She had white hair and a sharp nose and piercing gray eyes. I tried very hard to be good that year. On my first report card I got a C+ in overall conduct and a few Needs Improvement marks. But I also had more Satisfactorys than ever before. Then one fight, shortly after the Easter vacation, spoiled the whole year.

Maurice Fleetwood, or Bunny, as we used to call him, was afraid of everything. We got into an argument, I pushed him into the closet, and he began to cry and sniffle. A little snot bubble came out of his nose, and every time he took a deep breath, the bubble went into his nose, and every time he breathed out, it formed a bubble.

"Walter's going to give you a bloody nose," a girl said.

Bunny sniffled, the snot bubble grew large, and he swung at me. The punch was more out of fear than bravado, but it knocked me down.

Now the gathering crowd of kids started telling Bunny to run before I killed him.

Bunny couldn't get his legs going and, in a panic, swung at me again. This time I saw stars as I went flying backward. As I tried to get my eyes open, a girl pushed Bunny toward the door and he went half stumbling, half running away.

Mrs. Parker came in and called the class to order and asked what had happened. Naturally, she blamed me and told me that I had to bring my mother to school the next morning. Mrs. Parker couldn't leave well enough alone and kept telling the class what a bully I was. My left eye was swollen almost shut from where Bunny had hit me, and my stomach was cramping. As bad as I felt, I didn't need the extra burden of having the class turn and look at me while she made nasty remarks. I picked up my book and started looking at it.

"Put that book down!" she shouted.

I didn't put it down. I threw it. I meant to throw it into the corner to show how mad I was. She saw me getting ready to throw the book and jumped to one side. The book hit her on the shoulder, and she screamed.

"I want your mother here this afternoon, and when your mother gets here, I will have a police officer here to take you straight to reform school!" she screamed. "Put your head down on the desk at once. I don't want to see your face!"

I put my head down on the desk and tried hard not to cry. All year long I hadn't been in one fight in school and in only one or two outside of the school. Now I was going to reform school.

When school let out for lunch, I went home slowly. My stomach was really cramping up, and by the time I got up to the fourth floor, I was really miserable.

"What's the matter with you, boy?" Mama used the tone of voice that meant that she was serious.

"Nothing," I said.

I told her I wasn't hungry, and I lay down on the couch. Mama asked me if I was in any trouble in school. I had to tell her the truth.

"No."

She took me into the living room, put the radio on, and sat with me while I lay across the couch. Then I threw up. She helped me clean up, felt my forehead, and said that I had to go to the hospital.

Okay, that was different.

We went to the hospital, where a young doctor looked me over and asked me what was wrong. When I told him my stomach hurt, he asked me what I had eaten the day before. The day before had been the last day of Easter vacation, so I had tried to eat up most of the candy that was left over. He laughed and told my mother that I needed a laxative and I would be fine. Then a woman doctor who acted like his boss came in to check me. She didn't say anything as he told her what he thought was wrong. She reached under the sheet and pushed the lower right part of my abdomen. I screamed, and she turned to a nurse and told her to schedule an emergency operation. An hour later I was having my appendix removed.

When I got out of the hospital the next week, I got two books as presents, *The Bobbsey Twins at Spruce Lake* and *Mystery Rides the Rails*.

"By the time you finish these books, you'll be ready to return to school," said Mrs. Flynn, the principal at P.S. 125, who brought the books to Sydenham Hospital.

When I got home from the hospital, Mama was working again at a button factory she had worked in before. I was supposed to stay home and in bed. I could listen to the big radio, but I wasn't allowed to do anything strenuous, including going outside to play, until I had been cleared by the doctor. But I always had to be doing something. I had a very hard time sitting still and doing nothing. I would fill any space with some kind of physical activity. When I took my bicycle out and down the three flights of stairs to the street, I decided it would just be for a spin around the block.

I had been riding my bike for about an hour when I saw my father coming down the street. I rode across Morningside Avenue and struggled with the bike up the stairs as fast as I could. My belly hurt terribly from the effort, but I didn't want my dad to know I had disobeyed him and gone outside. I got the bike into the house and barely made it to my bed before collapsing. Somehow I got my sneakers, socks, and other clothes off and got under the covers. When Dad came into the room, I pretended to be asleep, and he left.

An hour or so later Mama came home, and she looked at me and asked me if I wanted some ice cream that she had bought me. I said no, and she felt my forehead and noticed that it was damp.

"You feeling all right, boy?" Dad asked when he came into the living room.

Yes was my answer, and he asked me why I was curled up. He pulled back the cover and saw the blood oozing from my bandaged stomach. He picked me up and rushed me to the emergency ward.

The incision had opened, either when I was riding the bike or when I was getting it back upstairs.

"What happened?" a doctor asked.

"I fell," I said.

"There might be some internal bleeding" was the diagnosis, and I spent another night in the hospital.

Home again, and Mama quit her job to take care of me.

I didn't attend any more classes that year. In early June my sister Gerry took me to school, but after a hurried conference between Mrs. Parker and Mrs. Flynn, I was promoted to the fifth grade and moved to a new school.

Bad Boy

The summer of 1947 was one of eager anticipation for black people across the country. Jackie Robinson and Larry Doby, two black players from the all-black Negro Leagues, had finally been accepted into major-league baseball. Joe Louis was heavyweight champion of the world, and "Sugar" Ray Robinson was the welterweight champion. The president, Harry S. Truman, was negotiating with black leaders to integrate the armed forces. The *New York Amsterdam News*, our local weekly Negro newspaper, suggested that the United States was now going to treat Negroes as equals for the first time.

Most of my life revolved around school and church. The schools I went to were integrated, and the church always had whites involved in some capacity. Like many black youngsters raised in northern cities, I was not aware of a race "problem" other than what I heard from older black people and an occasional news story. In sports, the area in which I was most interested, there seemed to be a good representation of blacks. Sugar Ray Robinson would drive slowly through the neighborhood in his brightly colored Cadillac and yell at us if we didn't get out of the street fast enough. We knew if we yelled back, he would jump out of his Caddy and box with two or three of us at once. Occasionally I would see Joe Louis walking slowly, almost majestically, along 125th Street.

Outside school and church there were the endless street games on 122nd Street. The block was safe to play on under the watchful eye of housewives who sat in the windows in the summer, catching whatever breeze there was in those days before air-conditioning. Women would sit in the windows, their arms folded before them resting on pillows used exclusively for street watching. Nothing would go on that they would miss.

A number of unexpected people entered my life that summer. The first was George Myers, my biological father, who had left West Virginia and settled in an apartment with his new wife and family in Harlem, a short distance from me. I knew that I had been adopted, although there had never been official proceedings to make the adoption legal. In the black community, as well as the white, extended families were common. Sometimes names were changed and sometimes, as in my case, they weren't. In school I was known as Walter Milton Myers. The neighbors, knowing my parents were the Deans, often referred to me as Walter Dean. I preferred Walter Myers for the most logical reason: If you wrote out the initials WM and turned them upside down, they were still WM.

I knew that George Myers existed and that he lived somewhere other than in New York. I don't remember ever having a feeling that I was his son, or that he was my father, but I was curious to see him and the other children who were to be my newly discovered brothers and sisters.

George Myers was a smallish, brown-skinned man who wore thick glasses. He greeted me formally and shook my hand, which I liked. I met his wife, Tommy. The oldest boy, also named George, was my full brother, and he was the same light color I was. He was called Mickey.

Mickey had slightly reddish hair that was straighter than mine. He was about my height despite the fact that I was two and a half years younger. We hit it off very quickly, and he was clearly glad to have a friend in his new and, for him, very strange city. It soon became clear to me that George Myers was not as well off as the Deans, probably because of the size of his family. Besides Mickey there was a set of twins, Horace and Harriet, and a girl, Gloria.

I knew I had three other full sisters — Gertrude, Ethel, and Imogene — who were not living in New York, and I was beginning to sort out my complex family ties. The woman who had given birth to me had had five children, of which I was the next to last, fitting in between Mickey and Imogene. These were my full siblings. The others were my half sisters and brothers. In effect, however, although I was not biologically related, I was raised in the Dean household as the baby of the family, and considered the Deans to be my "real" family.

The other person who now entered my life was my uncle Lee, finally out of jail. He looked a lot like my adoptive father, Herbert Dean. Uncle Lee had a habit of talking out of the side of his mouth. I asked him why he did that.

"So the screws can't see you talking," he said.

The who?

He explained that the screws were the prison guards. He had been in jail so long that talking out of the side of his mouth just came naturally. Just as naturally, I started talking out of the side of my mouth.

Mama restricted my activities that summer because of my having had my appendix out. I also didn't get any beatings that summer for the same reason. Not that I really deserved any, because there was only one thing I did that remotely suggested that I was on the wrong track. Richard Aisles (whose son turned out to be a fine trumpet player and jazz musician) lived in the next building. Richard had hurt his eyes by staring at the sun, which provoked the other kids on the block. Johnny Lightbourne, a boy close to my age, suggested we beat him up, but then we read in the *Amsterdam News* about a black man in the South who had been lynched by hanging. So we decided to hang Richard.

We took Richard down into the church basement, threw a rope over the railing that ran around the gym, and were stringing him up when Reverend Abbott came along. Reverend Abbott was a young white minister from Georgia who was assigned to our church for the summer. When he caught us lynching Richard, he turned about five shades whiter.

"You can't — that's — I don't believe . . ." He sputtered on and on. I guessed he had come from an area of the country where being lynched meant something a lot more serious than we knew about.

He went to each of our homes and told our mothers, who were unimpressed with our ability to hang Richard. Then he made us whitewash a wall, which was interesting, as none of us had ever done that before, and we proceeded to get whitewash all over ourselves. Even if I hadn't still been recuperating from my appendectomy, I don't think I would have received a beating for a simple hanging.

Beatings came easily in our neighborhood. None of our parents, with the possible exception of Robert Boone's mom, minded tearing our butts up. My mother used to tell me that she was going to do such a job on my particular butt that I would have to go down to Macy's to buy a new behind. The Boones were ultra-light-skinned blacks who had professional jobs and were upward bound. Light skin was a definite plus in our community, and it was common to talk in a negative manner about a person with very dark skin.

Beatings were not considered abuse. Black families, often working very hard to make ends meet, wanted to clearly define which behavior was acceptable and which was not. There was precious little anger involved with a beating, just a lecture explaining why you were getting one and why it was good for you. When there was nothing else to do, and we heard somebody was going to get a beating, we might even go so far as to gather around his door to hear it. Each kid knew just what he would get a beating for. At my house, a red conduct mark on my report card meant a beating. A note that said my mother had to go to school to see about my behavior meant a beating. Everything else resulted in a backhand lick, a warning, or being sent to my room.

By September and the opening of school I was deep into sports and became a baseball fanatic. Along with the pleasure of playing baseball there was the joy of identifying with the ballplayers. I loved the Dodgers. Maybe it was because Mama loved the Dodgers and especially Jackie Robinson. All summer long, kids playing punchball — hitting a pink "Spaldeen" ball with your fist and then running bases drawn in chalk on the streets — had tried to steal home to copy Robinson. We even changed the rules of stoop ball, of which I was the absolute King of the World, to include bases when more than one kid played. You played stoop ball by throwing the ball against the steps of a brownstone. The ball coming off the steps had to clear the sidewalk and land in the street. If it landed before being caught, you could run the bases. My speed and ability to judge distances made me an excellent fielder. We did occasionally play actual baseball, but not enough kids had gloves to make a good game.

My new school was Public School 43 on 128th Street and Amsterdam Avenue, across from the Transit Authority bus terminal. Mrs. Conway was my teacher, and it took me one day to get into trouble with her.

In the elementary grades I attended, reading was taught by having kids stand up one at a time and read aloud. Mrs. Conway had us up and reading as soon as the readers had been handed out. When it came to be my turn, I was anxious to show my skills. I read quickly, and there was a chorus of laughter in response. They were laughing at my speech.

"Slow down and try it again," Mrs. Conway said.

I slowed my speech down and started reading from the top of the page. Johnny Brown started laughing immediately. Johnny always had something to say to make the class laugh. I threw the book sidearm and watched it hit his desk and bounce across the room.

"Don't you dare throw a book in my classroom!" Mrs. Conway, red-faced, screamed. "Into the closet! Into the closet!"

I had to stand in the closet for the rest of the morning. That afternoon Mrs. Conway divided the class into reading groups. I was put into the slowest group. I stayed there until the next week, when the whole class was given a spelling test and I scored the highest grade. Mrs. Conway asked me to read in front of the class again.

I looked at Johnny Brown as I headed for the front of the class. He had this glint in his eye, and I knew he was going to laugh. I opened my mouth, and he put his hand across his mouth to hold his laugh in. I went across to where he sat and hit him right on the back of the hand he held over his mouth. I was sent to the principal's office and had to stay after school and wash blackboards. Later in the year it would be Johnny Brown who would be in Mrs. Conway's doghouse for not doing his homework, with her screaming at him that he couldn't be a comedian all his life. He went on to become a television comedian and is still doing well.

Being good in class was not easy for me. I had a need to fill up all the spaces in my life, with activity, with talking, sometimes with purely imagined scenarios that would dance through my mind, occupying me while some other student was at the blackboard. I did want to get good marks in school, but they were never of major importance to me, except in the sense of "winning" the best grade in a subject. My filling up the spaces, however, kept me in trouble. I would blurt out answers to Mrs. Conway's questions even when I was told to keep quiet, or I might roll a marble across my desk if she was on the other side of the room.

The other thing that got me in trouble was my speech. I couldn't hear that I was speaking badly, and I wasn't sure that the other kids did, but I knew they often laughed when it was my turn to speak. After a while I would tense up anytime Mrs. Conway called on me. I threw my books across that classroom enough times for Mrs. Conway to stop my reading aloud once and for all.

But when the class was given the assignment to write a poem, she did read mine. She said that she liked it very much.

"I don't think he wrote that poem," Sidney Aronofsky volunteered.

I gave Sidney Aronofsky the biggest punch he ever had in the back of his big head and was sent to the closet. After the incident with Sidney, Mrs. Conway said that she had had quite enough of me and that I would not be allowed to participate in any class activity until I brought my mother to school. I knew that meant a beating. That evening I thought about telling Mama that the teacher wanted to see her, but I didn't get up the nerve. I didn't get it up the next day, either. In the meantime I had to sit in the back of the room, and no kid was allowed to sit near me. I brought some comic books to school and read them under my desk.

Mrs. Conway was an enormously hippy woman. She moved slowly and always had a scowl on her face. She reminded me of a great white turtle with just a dash of rouge and a touch of eye shadow. It was not a pretty sight. But somehow she made it all the way from the front of the room to the back, where I sat reading a comic, without my hearing her. She snatched the comic from me and tore it up. She dropped all the pieces on my desk, then made me pick them up and take them to the garbage can while the class laughed.

Then she went to her closet, snatched out a book, and put it in front of me.

"You are," she sputtered, "a bad boy. A very bad boy. You cannot join the rest of the class until your mother comes in." She was furious, and I was embarrassed.

"And if you're going to sit back here and read, you might as well read something worthwhile," she snapped.

I didn't touch the book in front of me until she had made her way back to the front of the class and was going on about something in long division. The title of the book was *East o' the Sun and West o' the Moon*. It was a collection of Norwegian fairy tales, and I read the first one. At the end of the day, I asked Mrs. Conway if I could take the book home.

She looked at me a long time and then said no, I couldn't. But I could read it every day in class if I behaved myself. I promised I would. For the rest of the week I read that book. It was the best book I had ever read. When I told Mrs. Conway I had finished, she asked me what I liked about the book, and I told her. The stories were full of magic events and interesting people and witches and strange places. It differed from *Mystery Rides the Rails*, the Bobbsey Twins, and a few Honeybunch books I had come across.

I realized I liked books, and I liked reading. Reading a book was not so much like entering a different world — it was like discovering a different language. It was a language clearer than the one I spoke, and clearer than the one I heard around me. What the books said was, as in the case of *East o' the Sun*, interesting, but the idea that I could enter this world at any time I chose was even more attractive. The "me" who read the books, who followed the adventures, seemed more the real me than the "me" who played ball in the streets.

Mrs. Conway gave me another book to read in class and, because it was the weekend, allowed me to take it home to read. From that day on I liked Mrs. Conway.

I still didn't get to read aloud in class, but when we had a class assignment to write a poem, she would read mine. At the end of the year I got my best report card ever, including a glorious Needs Improvement in conduct.

It was also the golden anniversary of the school, and the school magazine used one of my poems. It was on the first page of the Jubilee Issue, and it was called "My Mother." When I saw it, I ran all the way home to show Mama.

Mr. Irwin Lasher

Harlem in the summer was and is an experience that will always live with me. I traveled, mostly with Mama, to other parts of the city, but nothing matched Harlem. Mama and I would occasionally go downtown to Macy's and Gimbel's or to the many stores along 14th Street, then a big shopping area. But neither 14th Street nor any other area had the colors of 125th Street. In Harlem the precise accents of northern-born blacks mixed with the slow drawls of recent southern immigrants and the lilting accents from the islands. Downtown, white people wore suits and white shirts to jobs in offices and stores. In Harlem, where the laborers lived, people wore the bright colors deemed inappropriate for offices.

Adam Clayton Powell, the pastor of Abyssinian Baptist, had led a protest that resulted in more black people working in the stores on 125th Street. Before his protests black people shopped on Harlem's main street but did not work there. As

61

more and more blacks found jobs in the stores, the character of the street changed. It became common to hear loudspeakers in the music stores fill the area with the sounds of jazz and to see strollers adjust their rhythms to the beat set down by Count Basie or even some gospel group.

Black businessmen walked side by side with black orthodox Jews. Uniformed members of Marcus Garvey's Universal Negro Improvement Association could be seen outside Micheaux's bookstore. White-dressed women, followers of the charismatic religious leader Father Divine, might be giving out leaflets. Even the white people who came to Harlem were colorful. In Smilen Brothers a bearded white man bent nails with his teeth and talked about the poisons in our foods. White nuns from St. Joseph's jostled with fat black women in Blumstein's for bargains, and the butchers in Raphael's meat market pushed slices of cold cuts across the counter for black children to nibble on while their mamas shopped.

The chief entertainment available to young people was the movies, and there were three major theaters along 125th Street. The Loew's showed first-run movies, as did the Alhambra. The Apollo, of course, was the showpiece of the community, with live entertainment as well as movies. Farther down the street the Harlem Opera House, which had once shown live performances when Harlem was mostly white, showed older films. The West End and Sunset each ran three movies and a number of shorts. Sometimes the West End would show a "colored" movie, one of the films made by black producers. There was also an arcade in which you could play games, have your picture taken, or even make a cheap plastic record of your voice. It was common for people just to walk along 125th Street as their evening's entertainment. What I knew about black people — or Negroes, which was the preferred term at that time — was primarily what I saw on 125th Street, in the newspapers, and in church. Blacks were entertainers, or churchgoers, or athletes. I decided I wanted to be an athlete.

There were two categories of friends in my life: those with whom I played ball and everyone else. Athletes were highly respected in the black community, and boys my age were encouraged to play some sport. I loved playing ball. I would play basketball in the mornings with the boys who were just reaching their teens, and then stoop ball or punchball on the block with boys my age. Sometimes Eric and I would go down to the courts on Riverside Drive and play there. And I was a bad, bad loser. Most of my prayers, when they weren't for the Dodgers, were quick ones in the middle of a game, asking God to let me win. I liked other sports as well and even followed the New York Rangers hockey team in the papers for a while until I found out that all the references to ice meant just that, that they were skating on ice. There wasn't any ice to skate on in Harlem, so I gave up following hockey.

With school out and me not having access to Mrs. Conway's cache of books, I rediscovered the George Bruce Branch of the public library on 125th Street. Sometimes on rainy days I would sit in the library and read. The librarians always suggested books that were too young for me, but I still went on a regular basis. I could never have afforded to buy the books and was pleased to have the library with its free supply.

Being a boy meant to me that I was not to particularly like girls. Most of the girls I knew couldn't play ball, and that excluded them from most of what I wanted to do with my life. Dorothy Dodson, daughter of the Wicked Witch, read books, and I knew she did, but she couldn't stand me and was more than happy to tell me so on a number of occasions. Sometimes I would see other children on the trolley with books under their arms and suspected that they were like me somehow. I felt a connection with these readers but didn't know what that connection was. I knew there were things going on in my head, a fantasy life, that somehow corresponded to the books I read. I also felt a kind of comfort with books that I did not experience when I was away from them. Away from books I was, at times, almost desperate to fill up the spaces of my life. Books filled those spaces for me.

As much as I enjoyed reading, in the world in which I was living it had to be a secret vice. When I brought books home from the library, I would sometimes run into older kids who would tease me about my reading. It was, they made it clear, not what boys did. And though by now I was fighting older boys and didn't mind that one bit, for some reason I didn't want to fight about books. Books were special and said something about me that I didn't want to reveal. I began taking a brown paper bag to the library to bring my books home in.

That year I learned that being a boy meant that I was supposed to do certain things and act in a certain way. I was very comfortable being a boy, but there were times when the role was uncomfortable. We often played ball in the church gym, and one rainy day, along with my brother Mickey and some of "my guys," I went to the gym, only to find a bevy of girls exercising on one half of the court. We wanted to run a full-court game, so we directed a few nasty remarks to the other side of the small gym. Then we saw that the girls were doing some kind of dance, so we imitated them, cracking ourselves up.

When the girls had finished their dancing, they went through some stretching exercises. A teenager, Lorelle Henry, was leading the group, and she was pretty, so we sent a few *woo-woo*s her way.

"I bet you guys can't even do these stretching exercises," Lorelle challenged.

We scoffed, as expected.

"If you can do the exercises, we'll get off the court," Lorelle said. "If not, you go through the whole dance routine with us."

It was a way to get rid of the girls, and we went over to do the exercises. Not one of us was limber enough to do the stretching exercises, and soon we were all trying to look as disgusted as we could while we hopped around the floor to the music.

They danced to music as a poem was being read. I liked the poem, which turned out to be "The Creation" by James Weldon Johnson. I liked dancing, too, but I had to pretend that I didn't like it. No big deal. I was already keeping reading and writing poems a secret; I would just add dancing.

The poems I wrote were mostly about finding rhymes to put on the ends of sentences, but I liked manipulating words, and I was doing it on a more-or-less regular basis. I read the poem I had published over and over. It was the first time I had seen my name in print, and it made me feel important. Mama had been so pleased, I wrote her a number of new poems, but none of them turned out as well as the first one had. I was disappointed, but I kept trying.

The summer between the fifth and sixth grades was going very well. Eric and I had become firm best friends. One of the local theaters put show cards in the window of his bakery and gave his father free passes. We went to all the movies and saw *Battleground* at least five times. He also told me a lot about the female anatomy. Apparently an older boy had given him the scoop, and he was only too eager to pass it on to me. For years I thought a girl might get pregnant if you touched her breasts. This was partially confirmed by my sister Gerry. Once, when she was chasing me with a chicken head, I turned and took a swing at her, hitting her on the breast. She told Mama, who told me never to hit a girl there. When Eric told me about girls getting pregnant, I figured that was what Gerry was worried about.

When Lorelle Henry and her group finally put on the dance recital, dancing and acting out "The Creation," with me in a central role as Adam and my brother, who couldn't dance, as a stiff-legged God, my father wouldn't come to see it. He didn't think young boys should be dancing around a stage in skimpy outfits. Mama came, and she said I did just fine.

Dad wasn't doing that well at U.S. Radium. I suspect the pay was just a bit over minimum wage, and I didn't get an allowance. If I wanted money, I would ask Mama, and she would give it to me if she had it. Then, on Saturday mornings, I began carrying packages for women at the A&P, sometimes earning as much as three dollars in a single day. When I earned that

68

much, I could go to the movies or go to a candy shop on 125th and buy a bag of stale candy for a dime. Also, there was a Chinese laundry on Eighth Avenue that sold used comics for a nickel, and I bought my share, sneaking them into the house rolled into my sock under a pants leg.

Except for the comics I spent most of the summer on the straight and narrow. Viola gave me a used book of Bible stories with dramatic illustrations. A librarian recommended some John R. Tunis books, mostly about baseball, which I liked.

My new school, the new P.S. 125, was quite close to my house. It was located on 123rd Street, right across from Morningside Park between Morningside and Amsterdam Avenues. The school was ultramodern for the day, with tables and chairs that could be arranged any way the teacher wanted instead of the rigid desks nailed to the floor we had been used to having. I was in class 6-2 and had my first male teacher, Mr. Irwin Lasher.

"You're in my class for a reason," he said as I sat at the side of his desk. "Do you know what the reason is?"

"Because I was promoted to the sixth grade?" I asked.

"Because you have a history of fighting

your teachers," he said. "And I'm telling you right now, I won't tolerate any fighting in my class for any reason. Do you understand that?"

"Yes."

"You're a bright boy, and that's what you're going to be in this class."

My fight with Mr. Lasher didn't happen until the third day, and in a way it wasn't really my fault. We were going up the stairs, and I decided that, when his back was turned, I would pretend that I was trying to kick him. All right, he paused on the staircase landing before leading us to our floor, and the kick that was supposed to delight my classmates by just missing the teacher hit him squarely in the backside. He turned quickly and started toward me. Before I realized it, I was swinging at him wildly.

Mr. Lasher had been in World War II and had fought in the Battle of the Bulge. He didn't have much trouble handling me. He sat me in a corner of the classroom and said that he would see me after class. I imagined he would send a note home, and that my mother would have to come to school. I was already practicing what I would say to her when I gave her the note. But instead of sending a note home, he came home with me! Down the street we came, my white teacher and me, with all my friends looking at me and a few asking if it meant I was going to get a beating. I thought it probably would, but I didn't give them the satisfaction of an answer. Mama was sitting on the park bench across from our house when I came down the street with Mr. Lasher firmly holding my hand.

"Mrs. Myers, I had a little problem with Walter today that I think you should know about," he said, sitting next to her on the bench.

He called Mama by my last name, not knowing that I was an informal adoptee. Her last name was Dean, of course, but she didn't go into it. Mr. Lasher quietly explained to my mother that all the tests I had taken indicated that I was quite smart, but that I was going to throw it all away because of my behavior.

"We need more smart Negro boys," he said. "We don't need tough Negro boys."

Mr. Lasher did two important things that year. The first was that he took me out of class one day per week and put me in speech therapy for the entire day. The second thing he did was to convince me that my good reading ability and good test scores made me special.

He put me in charge of anything that needed a leader and made me coach the slower kids in reading. At the end of the year I was the one student in his class whom he recommended for placement in a rapid advancement class in junior high school.

With Mr. Lasher my grades improved significantly. I was either first or second in every subject, and he even gave me a satisfactory in conduct. As the tallest boy in the sixth grade, I was on the honor guard and was scheduled to carry the flag at the graduation exercises, an honor I almost missed because of God's revenge.

I firmly believed that God saw everything and duly noted all transgressions, big and small. It was never my intention to do wrong, and so generally I thought I was in good stead with the Almighty. But as spring rolled around that year, I found myself barely hanging on to that side of the ledger.

I lived on Morningside Avenue, but I played mostly on the side streets because that's where the sewers were. The sewers were bases if you played stickball, they were the goal lines if you played football, they were the base if you played tag, they were the spot you made your first shot from if you played skullies. The side street between Morningside Avenue and Manhattan Avenue was a pleasant block, lined with brownstones that had been converted into either single-room occupancies with community bathrooms or, at least, apartment dwellings that contained between four and six families.

Few families on the side streets had refrigerators, and halfway down the block was a wooden pallet on which sat kegs of ice. You could ask the iceman for a fifteen-cent piece up to a dollar piece of ice (a dollar piece being absolutely huge). A thirty-five cent piece was big enough for a man with an ice shaver to buy and sell "icies," shaved ice with flavored syrup, and make a day's wage.

The whole block was guarded by Crazy Johnny, who had returned from the war shell-shocked. If anything went wrong, Crazy Johnny would try to set it right. This usually meant trying to stop fights between kids and sweeping up broken bottles.

We didn't get many yellow cabs coming to the street, because downtown cabs didn't stop for black people and you didn't need to use a cab when the A train came directly to Harlem. One day in May there weren't any kids on the block to play with except Clyde Johnson, who was too young to play with. A yellow cab pulled up in front of a building, and a fairly elegant looking lady got out. For some reason I thought it would be a good idea to hitch a ride on the back bumper of the cab. The cab started off with a jerk, and I was thrown off the bumper, but the sleeve of my shirt was caught. I was dragged the entire length of the block, bouncing along behind the cab, past the sewers, past parked cars, and all the way to the corner, where the cab was stopped by a light. It was there that I unhooked my sleeve and managed to get to my feet.

The agony was excruciating. Clyde asked me if I was hurt, and I said no.

"Your pants are torn," he said.

My jeans were in shreds at the knees, and the blood from my scraped knees was showing through. I tried to sit on the church steps, but the pain was too great. Stiff-leggedly I made my way around the corner and over to my building.

When I got home, Mama was on the phone and I went into the bathroom and got the iodine. Then I went to my room, stopping only to answer my mother's inquiry as to whether or not I was hungry.

"No, ma'am."

The iodine had a stopper and a glass rod applicator. I touched some iodine to my scraped leg. *Yow!* Enough of that. I went directly to bed.

When Mama called me for supper that evening, I called back that I wasn't hungry. She called me a second time and told me to come to the kitchen, where my father now sat at the table, his dinner before him. By that time my legs had stiffened so I could hardly walk.

"What's wrong with you, boy?" my father asked.

"Nothing." My universal answer.

"What's wrong with you, boy?" My father's voice again, deeper, more resolute.

"My legs hurt," I said.

"Take your pants down."

Right there at the dinner table. I had changed pants and now undid my belt and gingerly let the changed pants down. My mother gasped when she saw my legs — a mass of bruises, swelling, and dried blood.

"What happened to you?" my father demanded.

I knew that hitching a ride on the back of a cab was wrong. And I had been trying so hard all year to be good. Maybe all these things were swimming around in my head too quickly. I honestly don't know what

75

made me answer the way I did.

"Mama beat me with a stick," I said, the tears already flowing.

I think that if my mama hadn't been so shocked at the condition of my legs, she might have been able to respond. As it was, I don't think that she could really believe what she was hearing. First, there was her darling boy come home a bruised and bloody mess, in itself enough to send her into a blind panic, and then the same darling boy claiming to have suffered his injuries at her hand.

Maybe I could have reversed myself, admitted what had really happened, if my father had not gone absolutely crazy with anger. He bellowed, "If you ever . . . how . . . why . . . If you ever touch him again I'll . . ." My father sputtered on and on. At this point Mama was crying. I was gingerly put into a hot bath to let my legs soak. I sat in the hot water and listened as my father berated Mama. It never occurred to him that I could be lying about such a thing. I went to bed and told God I was sorry.

The next two days I couldn't go to school. Mama brought me food and put it on a chair near my bed. She didn't say anything to me, just looked at me as if she had never seen me before.

Two weeks later I was as good as new. Mama had been instructed by my dad not to touch me, and by the redness in his eyes she knew he meant it. I avoided *her* eyes when she asked how I could do such a thing to her. When she asked me what had really happened, I didn't answer. But Mama forgave me as usual, and I focused instead on the coming graduation from the sixth grade. My father checked my legs once a week because he hadn't forgotten the incident. Neither had God.

Eight days before graduation. We were playing stickball on 122nd Street, and a foul ball went up on the flat roof over the church vestibule. There was a drainpipe that came from the main roof and down the side of the church. Reverend Abbott, when he had been at the church the summer before, had put barbed wire on the pipe to keep us from climbing it to get balls that went up there. We had ripped the wire down, and every kid on the block, girls included, could climb onto that roof. Up I went after the foul ball. Enter Crazy Johnny.

"Get down from there!" he half yelled, half growled in his Crazy Johnny kind of way.

I threw the ball down, but I didn't come down. What I did instead was taunt Crazy

Johnny from my perch. Johnny knew about the drainpipe and started climbing up after me. What Johnny didn't know was that I had a plan.

Eric and I had watched enough war movies to know that if we ever got into the army, we were going to go airborne. Jumping out of a plane was fairly easy. You jumped, your parachute opened, and you floated down. In order not to hurt yourself on landing, you bent your knees, landed on your heels, and fell to one side.

Up came Crazy Johnny. My friends below screamed. I waited by the edge of the roof of the one-story building. I let Johnny get halfway across the roof before I jumped, my legs together and slightly bent. I landed on my heels, and the pain was unbearable.

Patty Lee and John Lightbourne, friends who lived on Morningside Avenue, helped me to the church steps, where I sat for a while before going home. I wanted desperately to tell somebody about the pain in my heels, but what could I say so soon after lying about the first incident? Oh, yes, I jumped off a roof? Mama beat me on the heels with a stick? I suffered in silence for the next two weeks. Years later I found out I had sustained minor fractures to both feet.

I Am Not the Center of the Universe

By the summer of 1949 both Viola and Geraldine had moved out. Viola worked in electronics, and she and her husband, Frank, had bought a house in Queens. Geraldine moved up to 147th Street, within walking distance, with her husband, a Navy veteran named Norman, and I got my own room. I had begun to sense that there was a way for people to live, and that it was our individual responsibility to find that way. I sensed this, and I didn't see a need to think it through fully. I had already been given a set of rules to follow that assured me, at the very least, that I would somehow get into heaven. The basis of my beliefs was the conviction that there was a God in heaven who looked down on us with infinite concern. His son, Jesus, had taken us from the Old Testament's hell-fire and given us a very cool way of living best summed up by the idea of doing unto others as you would have others do unto you.

Next, I believed in a certain fairness. Over the long haul things would have a way of working themselves out toward an essentially good position.

I was also convinced that those values I was being offered in school were right in the truest sense of rightness, that they were what both the world and God wanted. By accepting those values, I imagined, I would move into a society that would find me as wonderful as I found it, and together we would have achieved the state of being good. But there was something else going on, and that was the idea that while I wanted to be good — and my idea of being good was a very tolerant one — I also wanted to be like other kids so I would have friends.

As I approached my twelfth birthday, I was nearly six feet tall and physically aggressive. I loved to run, to jump, to test my strength and speed against other boys. I didn't at all mind fighting, if necessary. I was very close to moving to the next level of athletic ability, a level at which I would be better than most kids my age and ready to play against older kids. But this also would move me away from the kids most likely to be in the same social circles I was in. If we had had more organized sports, this would have worked itself out, but we didn't, and so I had to find my own place in sports. Mr. Reese, who lived on the first floor in my building and managed a Negro team, thought I might be able to play baseball in a few years if the Negro Leagues were still around.

I was also a reader. Not just a reader, but someone hungry for books. I was completely comfortable alone in my room with a book, more comfortable than in any other situation. If the other boys on the block were now smaller than me physically and somewhat behind in their athletic ability, they were far behind in their literary skills. They might have been as good in math, or mechanical skills, but they were not even close in reading or in exploring new ideas. Those values that I was accepting in school — being a good reader, being a person willing to explore the great ideas — were actually serving to separate me from other kids my age. I didn't want to be apart from them. I wanted, needed, to connect with people who were close to my own age, and to be accepted by them. I didn't think much of how my moving into a world of books was also moving me away from my parents.

"What do you want for your birthday?"

my mother asked as the summer drifted into August.

"A glove," I said. "Or a ball."

Either one would have done. We played sandlot baseball and rarely had a ball that was not taped, or resewn so that it had a lump in it that gave it a natural curve when you threw it. Mr. Reese would always lend us a couple of old bats if we wanted to play, but balls were something else, because we kept knocking them out of the sandlot. Once the balls left the lot, they would, as if by design, search for a sewer to go down. My birthday, the twelfth of August, fell on a Friday, and the plan was to have a party for me on the next day. It was to be my first birthday party, and I was looking forward to it.

What could Mama have thought of me that year? She had been through so much because of me. I had lied about her hitting me after the taxi incident. I had been involved in a few fights (duly reported by Mrs. Dodson) that upset her. But I had also graduated from the sixth grade at the top of my class and had been put into the special class for bright kids, and somehow Mr. Lasher had convinced the school officials that I deserved the award for Outstanding Boy.

"I was so proud of you carrying the flag," Mama had said after my graduation exercises. "You looked like you were walking on your toes down the aisles."

Of course, I had been walking on my toes because walking on my heels was impossibly painful due to my jump off the church roof. Mama wanted to reward me for doing well and had saved what money she could to pull together a party. It was with great anticipation that I went to sleep on Friday, knowing that I was now twelve and that the next day I would have both the party and the presents. I went to bed dreaming of getting a glove and a ball and perhaps a bat as well. Who knew?

I was awakened early in the morning by my mother.

"Walter, get up," she said. "I've got bad news. Your uncle Lee was killed last night."

We piled into the old Buick and made our way to the Bronx, where Aunt Nancy now lived. The apartment was cluttered with little porcelain figures, decorative plates, and ashtrays from various night-clubs. When we arrived, my aunt was crying loudly, her face contorted with grief. I had never seen that much sadness before, and the smells that permeated the apartment — liniment smells, stale tobacco, a pot of pepper rice and cloves on the stove — added a heavy weight to the atmosphere. My dad wanted to know if they were sure, and Aunt Nancy said she had been to the hospital. They were sure it was Uncle Lee. My father wanted to go and see for himself. I stayed behind as Dad, Mama, and several cousins went to the morgue.

I hadn't been that close to Uncle Lee, and in truth his death didn't mean that much to me. My father, however, was devastated. Uncle Lee hadn't been out of jail that long, and although he came to the house on more or less a regular basis, I never saw evidence of the closeness between them. They had lived together in Baltimore as kids, had struggled to survive, and had achieved a physical and emotional toughness that seemed to fit them well.

When Dad got back from the morgue, he looked like a stranger to me, wild-eyed and nearly incoherent. A cousin lit some incense in a brass holder, and the new scent drifted in thin wisps of smoke toward the yellowed ceiling. I learned that Uncle Lee had been drinking in a bar, had probably been drunk, and was robbed and beaten in an alley. He had been literally stomped to death, dying of internal injuries. My father cried openly, and I saw that Mama kept a short distance from him, almost as if she were afraid of his crying, as if the sudden grief had turned her husband into a stranger. In many ways it would do exactly that.

The funeral was filled with pain, open and naked and shared by my father and his sisters. Cousins and nephews and nieces prepared food and moved silently through the apartment in which the funeral was staged. The trip to the cemetery, the family praying, a strange woman singing "Precious Lord," were unfamiliar rituals. I had never seen adults crying before, their faces distorted and strained with emotion, their hurt pushing them awkwardly from the cars to the graveside and back, and then back to the Bronx, where they sat around the table, thinking tortured thoughts of what might have been if Uncle Lee had only had a few more years.

On the way home from the Bronx to Harlem, I saw that life went on. Kids were playing ball on 122nd Street, the iceman was delivering ice, women sat in the windows watching the world go by. Someone died, and life went on. Only Uncle Lee would not be a part of it.

The following Sunday morning, when I came out of my room and started talking,

Dad put his fingers to his lips. "This is Sunday," he said. "The Lord's day."

I looked at Mama, and she looked away. There was a woman preacher, Miss Anna Tuell, on the radio. Dad sat listening to her, and sometimes he nodded his head as if he were agreeing with what she had to say. He did this all day Sunday and the following Sundays for the rest of the year. At night when he came home from work, he hardly spoke. He would eat and then listen to some church program — there seemed always to be one on the radio — until it was time to go to bed. The mourning depressed Mama something terrible and disrupted our lives. There were no longer just the three of us in the house. Dad's grief for his brother was as real as if it were a stranger who lived with us, a stranger who had taken my place in the center of the universe.

Dad's depression affected Mama a great deal, and I thought she became distant even when he wasn't around. Now, looking back, I think that it might have been I who had become distant as well. Death was new to me, an uncomfortable event that I did not fully understand. But my father was nearly impossible. Sometimes at night when I woke, I would hear him praying aloud as he knelt by the bed. I remember that once I heard my parents argue in the morning before Dad went to work. When he left, the door slammed. I asked Mama what had happened. Her eyes were red-rimmed, and she told me she couldn't stand my dad's sadness.

"Lee's dead," she said. "Not all of us."

Suddenly the world had stopped revolving around me. I was still a part of it all, playing ball, eating, reading, experiencing the death of a family member, and the sadness. But I was only a small part.

My father's depression lasted for an entire year. He turned to religion in a way that I had never seen before. He didn't speak much, and never went out. Christmas came and went that year with me and Mama sitting in the living room with the Christmas tree and Dad sitting in the kitchen by himself. What I missed most about him was his offbeat sense of humor. Before Uncle Lee's death my dad could find humor in almost any situation. Now there was nothing funny, nothing without the heavy shadow of his brother's death.

The term before, Mr. Lasher had recommended that I be put into a newly formed rapid advancement class, and I had taken the test to get in. Tests were always easy for me. I saw them as games, saw myself as being in a contest against a mythical adversary, and welcomed the challenge. Dorothy Dodson and Eric were also going to be in the class. The other kids came from all over the city, some from as far away as Brooklyn.

We were going to do the seventh and eighth grades in one year and were then going to do the ninth grade the next year, making up any work we needed along the way. The school we were going to was Junior High School 43, now Adam Clayton Powell Academy, on 128th Street. The class initially consisted of fourteen girls and eleven boys, a small class for the time. I was officially going to be considered "smart."

I liked the rapid advancement class, also called SP. SP stood for Special Progress, and all the kids in the class were indeed smart. For most of the year we spent our time studying each other. None of us had been around that many other kids who were so smart. It was a class in which everyone got a ninety on every test, and an eighty was a source of derision. But I also noticed, for the first time, a sense of being alone. While part of the feeling was because of my home situation, there was more to it than that.

In school we studied American history including, for the first time, slavery. Our discussion was the usual one for the time. Slavery, we were taught, was a distant and unfortunate period in American history and had led to the Civil War. In the history book there was an image of scantily clad Africans, their heads down, being marched off a boat under the watchful eyes of white men armed only with walking sticks. I was glad to get past the abbreviated reference to slavery. No one spoke the words, but I believe that every black kid in the class who, like me, thought that life was fundamentally fair must have felt on some level that those enslaved blacks had somehow *deserved* to be enslaved.

Mama, despite her being half German, half Indian, knew a lot about slavery. She had heard stories about the cruelties of slavery from the older black people around Martinsburg, West Virginia.

"They dug a hole when they wanted to beat a pregnant woman," Mama said. "They put her belly in the hole so they wouldn't hurt the baby."

When we had passed the two pages on which slavery was mentioned in the textbook, I moved away from it mentally as well. I remember noticing that Robert E. Lee's horse was named Traveller, the same name as my bicycle. The black kids in the class wanted to identify with the values we were being taught, and the concept of being slaves was a clear deflection of those values. The teachers didn't seem to notice that the black kids weren't comfortable with the textbook. They also didn't seem to notice anything wrong in our music class when we sang "My Old Kentucky Home," the version with the "darkies" being gay.

Ivanhoe, The Prince and the Pauper, and some poems by Kipling and Tennyson were among the things I read in school the first year in the special class. On my own I found *Tom Sawyer* and *Huckleberry Finn,* and my sister Geraldine gave me a copy of *Little Men.* I didn't like *Ivanhoe,* hated *The Prince and the Pauper,* tolerated the poems, and loved *Tom Sawyer* and *Huck Finn.* I also loved *Little Men* and, after reading it twice, got *Little Women* from the library. I thought *Little Women* was quite possibly the worst book ever written.

Although I was a reader, I did not associate books with writing. I liked to look at pictures of writers, and none of the writers whom I was studying in school had any relation to anything I knew as being real. They were all, as far as I knew, dead. Those who weren't dead were probably English, which meant about the same thing to me. That year I also discovered a book that alluded to sex. It was one of my better finds for the year.

When my mom was home, I would come home for lunch. When she was back working in the factory or cleaning apartments, she gave me money for lunch. I would use the money to buy adult paperbacks with girls on the cover. There weren't any real girls whom I particularly liked, although Dorothy Dodson was becoming interesting, but the idea of having a girlfriend appealed to me. So when, after a few months, the girls in the class made a ranking of all the boys according to which ones were "hunks," I was hopeful. The class had shrunk to ten boys, and I came out eighth. So much for girls. My grades were good, and our class basketball team, with Eddie Norton as captain, was the second best in the school. I was still taking speech therapy classes, but I wasn't fighting anymore.

What I was doing was spending more and more time alone in my room, reading or writing. Mama started playing the numbers, and I learned how to get the winning number from the radio by adding up the race results. Sometimes we watched television together, but more and more we did so in silence.

As the year wore on, my father made an effort to come out of his depression. Occasionally we would go out to Rockaway Beach, and he would fish off a jetty. Mama and I had no interest in fishing, and so we would walk along the beach. I liked the smell of the sea and the mystery of crabs scrambling onto the shore. Mama was just glad to get out of the apartment.

A Writer Observes

Harlem. As I grew older, I began to see things differently. At thirteen I wanted to see the world around me the way I thought a real writer would have seen it, full of magic and marvels and breathtaking beauty, which would inspire me to write the kinds of poetry I had read in school. I wanted to look at the world through the eyes of a Shelley or a Byron, to feel the inspiration that guided their pens. I didn't have a typewriter, and so I wrote everything in black-and-white covered composition books.

I had traveled to other parts of New York City, but my world, of course, was Harlem. Physically, Harlem was one of the most beautiful areas in the world. Bounded by Central Park to the south, and lying between the Hudson and East Rivers, it was built up in the 1890s as an ultramodern urban environment for middle- and upper-class whites. The expansion northward from the center of the city was too rapid, and the new housing, including elegant brownstones and magnificent apartments designed by the country's leading architects, was soon a money-losing proposition for the many investors. Soon apartments originally designed for one family were being cut up into two-and three-family dwellings, and blacks, who had been confined previously to the West Forties, were allowed to move in. By the First World War, the community was a ghetto in the making. Its residents' struggle to maintain their dignity despite absentee landlords and poor city services was intense and ongoing.

One morning I started my formal observations, beginning at 125th Street and the Hudson River. The Harlem part of the river was dotted with ancient wooden piers. Some older men were fishing off the end of the pier I went down, and a heavyset woman was lowering crab baskets over the side. I had brought romantic images of Mark Twain's Mississippi River with me when I went to the Hudson, but it wasn't to be. There were a few old boats moored on the next pier, one that looked like a coal scow, but nothing even vaguely romantic. I moved on eastward along 125th Street.

There was a milk-bottling plant, and I

watched the rows of milk bottles move relentlessly along a conveyor belt and tried to make a big deal of that. Not much there for the budding writer either. I was beginning to wonder what authors like Byron and Shelley were seeing, or if they were really just more sensitive to beauty and interest than I was. I moved on.

Still walking along 125th Street, I was seeing what I had seen all my life. I didn't know how to look at the sights with fresh eyes. The funeral parlor on the corner looked like the funeral parlor on the corner, the West End Theater, with its "THREE, 3, THREE BIG FEATURES, and a SERIAL," looked the same, as did the small stores along Harlem's central byway. It was early, and there were a few musicians with their instruments talking outside the Apollo. I tried to match them with the faces on the show cards outside the theater. Pegleg Bates, the one-legged tap dancer, was appearing, along with a band and a comedian.

I continued across 125th until I reached the building where Unity Insurance was located. Unity was where I went once every three months to make insurance payments for my parents. It was called life insurance but it was really burial insurance, to make sure that when the insurance holders died, they would at least have a decent funeral. One of the worst things that could be said about someone from Harlem was that he was buried in potter's field. It was as if his whole life was being summed up in those two words.

Harlem had wonderful rooftops, and sometimes I would take the stairs to ours to sit near the edge overlooking Morningside Avenue and read. When I got home after making my rather scanty "observations," I went up to the roof and decided to record what I saw on the street below. My aim, as I remember it, was to write something wonderfully dramatic. When it was warm, the sun would soften the tar, which gave off a distinctive odor. Sometimes people would barbecue on the roof, and more than once I had heard of parties where someone actually fell off, although I don't remember this ever being verified. Some roofs had clotheslines with white sheets flapping in the summer breeze. I liked being high above the world, and I spent a lot of time either on the roof or sitting in a tree in the park.

Across from me, on the park side, there were women with small children sitting on the park benches. I recognized some of the women, big-hipped and solid, whom I had seen sitting on those same benches since we had moved to the neighborhood. In the park, men were playing checkers. There were more children, running in seemingly aimless patterns while sparrows flew over-head, tracing the same pathways through the air.

When a Fifth Avenue bus passed, it was a double-decker, and I made notes comparing it to a huge yellow-and-green dragon, which it did not look like at all. A Studebaker passed, and I tried to make something of the fact that it looked the same from the front or back. That didn't work either. Maybe, I thought, I would have to move to the country, or at least to another part of the city. Harlem was not exotic, or special. Harlem was just home.

I decided to write about people I saw in the neighborhood.

Mrs. Dodson, the Wicked Witch of the West. Mrs. Dodson was a tall, brown-skinned woman with an intelligent, pleasant face anchored by a resolute lower lip that signaled that she would put up with no nonsense whatsoever. She had opinions, and if you dealt with her, you would deal with those opinions in no un-certain terms. Her husband, a big handsome man just slightly shorter than his wife, worked on the railroad and was gone for days at a time. Working on the railroad was considered a good job, and A. Philip Randolph, perhaps the most important figure in the civil rights movement, was making it a better job. But it was Mrs. Dodson, WW of the W, who ran that family. Her three children, Robert, Dorothy, and Helen, were going to do the right thing, and no one knew the right thing better than Mrs. Dodson. My only real quarrel with her was that she also thought she knew the right thing for me. Which she didn't.

Melba Valle lived above us and was a part-time model and dancer. She did flamenco dancing, and we could hear her heels pounding on the ceiling and the distinct clicking of castanets. My mom hated her. She would get a broom and bang on the ceiling. I secretly bought a pair of castanets and taught myself at least to emulate some of the sounds I heard from above. Melba made the cover of *Jet* magazine, a really big deal in the black community, and at least once was in a dance program with Geoffrey Holder. Years later, at Geoffrey's house, I asked him if he remembered her, and he said yes, but there was no obvious recognition on his face, and I wondered if he was just being polite. Melba had ambitions to be more than just someone who lived on the Avenue, and that attracted me to her. I also liked her warmth and openness, even to the kid who lived on the floor below. But there was a sadness to her as well. Many of the people in the building didn't like her, claiming that she tried to make herself different from the others. It was the first time I had heard about people trying to be "not just another Negro."

Bodie Jones was something else. I'm not even sure how to spell his first name. It could have been Bo "D" or some other variation. His dad or uncle played with Count Basie's band, and Bodie played trumpet as well. He was older than me and would make remarks about how I spoke. I always wanted to fight him, but he would back off (even though I'm sure he would have punched my lights out). One time he said, in front of Light Billy, Binky, and some other guys, that he was going to kick my tail. He put one hand in his pocket, suggesting that he had a knife. I wasn't afraid of his knife for two reasons; the first was that my brother Mickey was standing behind him holding a baseball bat, and the second was that I was kind of stupid.

Mickey and I had become friends. My adoptive parents gave me better circumstances than he had, at least to my way of thinking. Our biggest problem was that where he was laid-back, almost passive, I was very aggressive. Small disagreements for Mickey were reasons to move on to another subject; to me they were reasons to fight. He was also more constricted than I was. Mickey, for some reason, had to stay in our Harlem neighborhood. I would travel down to the Riverside Park boat basin, at 79th Street, on my bike, or up to the International House on Riverside Drive.

What impressed me most as an observer was the entrance to the A train on 125th Street and St. Nicholas Avenue. There were constant streams of people going down those stairs in the mornings and coming up them in the evenings. They were going downtown to jobs I knew about — jobs as laborers, cleaning people, messengers. I knew there were exceptions. The *Amsterdam News* and *Ebony* always printed pictures of blacks who worked in downtown offices or who had achieved some small recognition. But next to the accomplishments of whites, the stories about blacks in the *Amsterdam News* were almost silly. The white newspapers would have a story about some white senator making a speech, or some white businessman opening a branch office somewhere, and the black paper would have a story about a man who was given a certificate for having a job as elevator operator for twenty years. White singers performed at Carnegie Hall. If a black singer appeared at Carnegie Hall, it wouldn't be in an opera but in a recital, which would include Negro spirituals.

The idea that race played a large part in the life process was becoming clear to me. I knew that blacks did not have the same chances as whites, and I did not want to do something that was commendable only as a Negro accomplishment. I wanted whatever I managed to do in my life to reflect the core values I was learning in school, in my church, and in my community. What I was doing, without knowing it, was accepting the idea that whites were more valuable than blacks. I knew I would never be white, and therefore I wanted to be without a race.

My role models for writing were the ones we learned about in school. If an Englishman could appreciate beauty, why couldn't I? If

Shakespeare could write about love and jealousy and hatreds, why couldn't I? At thirteen I had never read a book by a Negro writer. Perhaps they had some at the George Bruce Branch, but I didn't want to identify myself as a Negro by asking.

After my frustrating time of trying to write about my neighborhood the way I had seen other published authors write about theirs, I stopped writing for a while. I had never thought much about just being a Negro, or what that meant. I began to suspect that, if I were not careful, in all likelihood I would one day be relegated to taking the A train downtown, as my father did and as occasionally Mama did, to clean up for some white person.

In school the boys in my class started a club. The idea of the club was to be as macho as possible and to establish once and for all that we were something special. Across the street from the school was a bus terminal. They printed transfer pads at the terminal, and it was no problem for us to sneak into the terminal past the old man whose job it was to keep us out, and get a few transfers, or even a whole pad of them, from the printing-room floor. Then we would wait for the bus that stopped in front of the school, present the transfers, and ride the few blocks to the subway. It was a very small but very gratifying triumph. One afternoon at lunchtime five of us made our way into the terminal and up to the roof garage. For some reason, instead of looking for transfers, we were going to sit in a bus. Then it was decided, I think by James Williams, that we would see if we could start the bus. Getting the bus started was easy, and we decided to take it for a spin around the garage roof. James, our designated driver, got the bus out of its space and a quarter of the way past the rows of parked vehicles when we heard the police whistle.

James stopped the bus, and the guys bolted toward an exit. I was sitting in the back of the bus, feet up and over the back of the seat in front of me, and so I was the last one out. I saw my classmates run through the exit and make a sharp right. Knowing that if the police did chase us, they would probably chase the largest segment, I broke off and turned left, right into the arms of the first police officer.

We were all rounded up and put against the wall. The old man who had called the police was the same one whom we had constantly bedeviled as we snatched transfer pads earlier that week.

"Yes, that's them!" he shouted gleefully, "Where's the big white one?"

He was looking for Eric, who had gone home for lunch. The police took our names and classroom number and said they would pick us up that afternoon.

Back in class we were obviously upset and told the girls what had happened. Every time the door opened, five hearts nearly stopped beating. Stephanie Bena, the smartest person I had ever met in my entire life, asked to go to the bathroom. Ten minutes later she returned, opened the door, and shook her head sadly.

"Here they are, officer," she announced in a loud voice as she looked down the hallway.

If Jonathan Willingham hadn't started crying on the spot, I would have. Our teacher, Mr. Siegfried, turned to see what was going on, and Stephanie, having properly scared every one of the guilty five to death, smiled, closed the door, and took her seat.

At the end of the year there was another incident, this time away from the school, that was to have a major effect on me. An Irish kid named Eddie was having a party. He asked Eric to come and told Eric that he could bring anyone he wanted. Eric asked me in front of Eddie if I wanted to come to the party. I said yes. Later Eddie told Eric that I couldn't come because I wasn't white.

Eric was mad and told me that I should beat the crap out of Eddie. I wanted to do just that, but I was more hurt than I was mad.

Sonnets from the Portuguese

The seventh and eighth grades, which our Special Progress class did in one year, were remarkable only in that I had no major fights and for the depression of my father. I ended the year glad to be released from the hot classrooms but with few prospects for the summer. I had fewer friends than ever, having lost anything of common interest with the boys on my block who were my age. Boys slightly older were moving on to girls and dating and fitting in with the mores and restrictions of being in their mid teens, which meant, among other things, avoiding associations with younger boys. I was twelve and going into the ninth grade of what would today be called a "gifted" program, while many of the other kids my age were just going into the seventh. The only sport I was playing now was basketball, often with guys four or five years older than I was.

Basketball was very satisfying. It gave me

a chance to compete, which I loved, and it was highly respected in the community. A good basketball player would be known throughout Harlem. Beyond the idea of winning, which was important to me, I liked the physical aspects of playing ball. Going up for a rebound and snatching it off the backboard over an opponent was a thrill. To even get into one of the tough summer tournaments, with players coming from as far away as Philadelphia, was sheer delight.

My sister Imogene had come to Harlem to live with George Myers. She was bright, beautiful, and feisty, but, like Mickey, she was not allowed out of the house that much. I wanted her to see me play ball in the worst way, but she could never get to the better games that I managed to play in. I did show her some of my poetry, which she liked. I thought Jean, as we called her, was a lot like me and began wondering more often what my biological family was like.

Mr. Lasher had convinced me that I was bright, and by the time I approached the ninth grade, education had become very important to me. There was far less pretense in the New York City school system than there is today. High schools were divided into four general categories: vocational, commercial, general, and academic. Only 25 percent of all male students attended academic high schools and were expected to go on to college. The rest, even if they did graduate from high school, were expected to take their place in the workforce immediately. The dropout rate was quite high, but it didn't seem to matter all that much. Most jobs could be handled by anyone with a willingness to work and some reading ability. But I knew that a poor education would probably land me in a "Negro" job, that lower level of employment in which so many of the neighborhood men seemed to be hopelessly stuck.

By this time there were two very distinct voices going on in my head, and I moved easily between them. One had to do with sports, street life, and establishing myself as a male. It was a fairly rough voice, the kind of in-your-face tone that said I wouldn't stand for too much nonsense either on the basketball courts or in the streets. The other voice, the one I hid from my street friends and teammates, was increasingly dealing with the vocabulary of literature. Harlem had a rich literary heritage of which I knew nothing. The so-called Harlem Renaissance, which produced writers such as Langston Hughes, Claude McKay, Zora Neale Hurston, and Countee Cullen, had ended during the Depression of the thirties, and none of these writers were taught in city schools. Moreover, there were few black librarians. I remember none in the George Bruce Branch who might have recommended any of these writers to me.

I spent the summer with my time divided between playing basketball and reading. In ball I was helped briefly by a thin black man called Fatty who was the coach of a team called the Comanches, one of the best teams in the city. He talked to me about the possibility of playing ball in college, and I was encouraged. When I wasn't playing ball, I read everything I could get my hands on. The reading was largely indiscriminate. At the library, I would pick up a novel, read a page or two, then make a quick decision as to whether or not I wanted to borrow it. When a librarian at the George Bruce commented that I probably wasn't reading all the books I took out, I began to space out my visits. I wanted her to think that I was a reader.

Mary Finley was our teacher in the ninth grade. Never have I seen a teacher with such high hopes or one who would be so bitterly disappointed. The class had been together for a year, and she was the outsider. The first week of the new term set the tone for the whole year. Leon Sadoff's father ran a kiosk on Amsterdam just off 125th Street, and we got nine plugs of chewing tobacco from him. The idea was hatched during one morning, the plugs acquired at lunchtime, and the chewing began right after lunch. None of us had ever chewed tobacco before, and why we thought it was a good idea is beyond me to this day. I can't remember the first boy who threw up, but I do remember Mrs. Finley's face when the rest of us started spitting out our tobacco wads. The class, in the middle of a history lecture, broke down into a group of retching, spitting thirteen-year-old boys, with the girls retreating to the open windows for air. Mrs. Finley was on the verge of tears and absolutely speechless. Her dismay, along with the disgust of the girls, made the whole venture worthwhile even as we had to clean up the mess we made with rags and buckets of water brought up by the cleaning staff.

Mrs. Finley tried to minimize the damage by saying that one of the boys had become ill and made the others sick. But the next week there was a spitball fight in our typing class, which blew our cover. The girls, after the tobacco incident, were somewhat envious of our notoriety. When Mr. Goldstein, the typing teacher, left the room and the spitball fight started, the girls joined in with a vengeance. Mr. Goldstein was not amused when he returned to see the typing room, including his desk, covered with spitballs.

The word quickly got around the school that the SP students were troublemakers, and Mr. Manley, our French teacher, explained to us in no little detail how disgusting we were and what an educational opportunity we were wasting. Mr. Manley was also the only black teacher we had.

Mrs. Finley was our homeroom teacher and also taught English. I thought she was boring. Boring, that is, until we came to the sonnets of Elizabeth Barrett Browning. We had read sonnets before, but Mrs. Finley, reading Browning's poems, gave them new meaning.

If thou must love me, let it be for naught
  Except for love's sake only. Do not say,
"I love her for her smile . . . her
  look . . . her way
  Of speaking gently — for a trick of
  thought. . . ."

Mrs. Finley introduced us first to the life of Elizabeth Barrett. Here was a sickly woman who lived much of her life alone and who wrote poetry from the time she was a child. The poems we read in class were her expressions of love to Robert Browning, her husband. The poetry was personal, and I was able to understand it as a personal expression by the writer rather than as what had seemed to me to be the impersonal writing of the earlier poems I had read. Perhaps someone could be so moved by a Grecian urn that he would instantly sit down and write a poem about it, but the idea of writing to someone you loved was immediately attractive to me. The poetry had come *from* Browning as well as being written by her.

Sonnets from the Portuguese used form and meter with an ease and grace that I envied. I wanted to write like Elizabeth Barrett Browning. I wanted to sit by my window, my small dog on my lap, and write this intensely personal poetry. The sonnet form allowed me to make my poems look and feel like real poetry without being as distant as some of the other British poetry I had read.

Mrs. Finley assigned us the task of writing a sonnet. I wrote dozens of sonnets.

Mrs. Finley told me to put them into a notebook, and I did, writing them first on scrap paper and then, when they were as perfect as I needed them to be, carefully copying them out into my poetry notebook.

She took us from the sonnets of Browning to the sonnets of Shakespeare, which I found difficult. Where Browning was straightforward and usually clear, Shakespeare was devious, never being quite where you wanted him to be. When the class complained about how difficult it was to read Shakespeare's sonnets, we were challenged to learn enough to understand his references, and to be mentally alert enough to see his puns and his layers of ideas. I tried writing a few poems à la Shakespeare, but quickly returned to Browning.

That Christmas, Mrs. Finley gave me paperback copies of both the comedies and tragedies of Shakespeare.

As the holiday season neared, my dad seemed finally to shake his blues. On his payday we drove downtown to Division Street and bought presents for my sisters, and he actually kidded around with Mama. She pretended to be annoyed, but I knew she was greatly relieved. So was I.

After Christmas we read more British poetry. To many of my classmates Mrs. Finley's dramatic readings of the English poets were comical, and I went along with laughing at her, but secretly I wanted to be an English poet. I wrote more sonnets and odes to everything imaginable. "Ode to the Summer Rain." "Ode to a Leafy Sycamore Tree." "Ode to a Church Steeple." I was filling more and more notebooks.

The prints we saw of Shelley and Byron were of ethereal young white men with flowing hair. Mrs. Finley made them sound as if they were naturally brilliant, and I studied the images, trying to discern who they were. It was clear they were like no one I had ever known.

Each class had to do an assembly program for the entire school. Our first effort was a Japanese play called *The Stolen Prince*. The play was in Noh form. A narrator told the story but the actors were silent. A property man, dressed in black, moved items around the stage, concealed by his dark clothing, lighting, and the imagination of the audience. In *The Stolen Prince* I was the property man, and I also played a pennywhistle, in an imitation of Japanese music, for atmosphere.

This was a class of fiendishly bright kids

who knew just how bright they were. Mrs. Finley wanted us to behave like the young scholars she imagined us to be. We wouldn't. We behaved badly at every turn and received more class reprimands than any other class in the school's history. Kids wouldn't move to the right places during rehearsals, or would ad-lib wisecracks, which Mrs. Finley didn't think at all funny. On the day we were to perform the play, she was virtually in tears. The play she saw as a gentle incursion into another culture we played as a comic romp with great effect. The school principal, who knew of our bad behavior reports, had come to the play and loved it. We were asked to perform it two more times.

Sometime during the school year we had to choose which high school we wanted to attend. The only boy who had an idea of which school he wanted to go to was Edward Norton, whose brother, John, went to Stuyvesant High School. The five guys on the class basketball team, including my friend Eric, took the test for Stuyvesant, and we all passed.

The next play we did for assembly was an enactment, totally adapted by Mrs. Finley, I believe, of *The Rime of the Ancient Mariner.* The whole class had to memorize the poem, and we were all assigned roles. Roberto Lembo, who took dance classes after school, did the choreography.

The Coleridge poem gave me yet a new idea about writing. *The Rime of the Ancient Mariner* did not have the elegance of any of the sonnets we had read, nor did it have the soaring language of a poem by Shelley or Byron. It was poetry designed to tell a tale. When we were in the seventh/eighth grades, Mr. Siegfried had read with us some narrative poetry that told of historical events (most notably "The Charge of the Light Brigade"), but the Coleridge epic had something more. It had a symbolism that wasn't in the other poems, and it also involved the poet's ideas about the moral responsibility of the mariner. He was the one who had shot the albatross, and yet in the end we pitied him. I was learning how many ways poetry could have meaning.

A few years later, sailing in Arctic waters similar to the ones that Coleridge described, I was surprised to find out that some of what I had considered to be merely fancy writing by Coleridge were actually fairly accurate descriptions of natural phenomena.

Mrs. Finley was one of the few teachers I felt sorry for. She was willing to give so much more than we were willing to take.

At the end of the year she reminded us of how bright we all were and how it was our responsibility to do something with that brightness. The school's opinion of the experiment with the special classes for bright kids was clearly negative, she explained. We had made light of all the advantages we had been given and had treated the school with disdain, or so it seemed. But I also think that all the kids in that SP class took away something very special, the notion that each of us had intellectual gifts to spend as we chose.

While I had moved more into writing, and into reading, I was moving further and further away from my parents. I did write some poems which I showed my parents. Mama said they were nice and asked me to explain one of them, which I did. She said that my dad had liked them too. I was disappointed. I think I wanted to hear him, in his kindness, say the words.

What I did not know about my father was that he couldn't read.

Heady Days at Stuyvesant High

The idea of what it means to be poor changed in the late sixties, when American manufacturers began to import their products from overseas and we began to accumulate "things." Prior to that, it seems to me, we thought about being well off or not well off in terms of personal comfort or distress. If your circumstances were such that you couldn't afford to eat, or have a home, or have clothes to wear, then you were poor. My dad worked as a laborer, and we didn't have much, but I was never hungry in my life. That was the case with most of my friends, and we didn't mind collecting cans of food to send to the starving kids of Wherever Starving Kids Were Hanging Out.

My family had burial insurance on all of us. We were on good terms with Mr. Richards, the landlord, so even if we had to have him come back the next week for the rent, he didn't mind. Each year my parents would go across town to Household Finance and borrow money for Christmas. This, along with the annual Christmas bonus, would get us through the holidays in fine spirits, and throughout the year we would make weekly repayments. The holidays were important, and the discipline needed to pay for the pleasure of annual generosity was relatively painless. Mama always used to say that she would buy some needed thing "as soon as I can spell Able." Because we had spent so little money during my father's mourning for his brother, we managed to clear up the Household Finance bill earlier than expected, and it truly looked as if we were on the verge of "spelling Able." But like most families in Harlem we could not tolerate unexpected financial burdens, and in the summer of 1951 we experienced two. I was the first.

Most of my life until then had been divided between school, reading, and ball playing. School was free, as was reading when the books were from the library, and the only thing needed to play basketball in Harlem were sneakers and a game. I had both. But I had grown to six feet and had the appetite of a growing teenager. A head taller than my father, I was wearing clothing that would fit only a larger man. My family had had to borrow the money for the suit in which I graduated from the ninth grade. There was little money to outfit me for high school, and there were few jobs available to a fourteen-year-old. On weekends I hustled in front of the A&P, carrying packages for women, and sometimes I ran errands for neighborhood people. I used the money I made just to have something in my pocket in case Eric or my brother Mickey wanted to go to the movies.

The second burden of that summer came in the form of my grandfather. The Department of Welfare in Baltimore contacted my father and said that William Dean, his father, had lost most of his sight and needed welfare assistance. But since he had a working son, he could receive only a small portion of what he would get if he had no living relatives. My father would have to send him money on a regular basis or send for him. My father decided that it would be better to bring his father to live with us.

William Dean was a tall, ramrod-straight man with mannerisms that seemed more appropriate for the nineteenth century than for 1951. His father had been born a slave in Virginia and had risen to the position of overseer. After the Civil War the former slave stayed on as plantation boss. His son William moved to Baltimore as a young man and did odd jobs until he could establish himself in a hauling business, eventually owning his own company with several teams of horses and a number of wagons. It was typical of him, or at least I thought so, that he had made the decision that horses could never be replaced by the newfangled trucks.

When he arrived at 81 Morningside Avenue, he seemed in good health except for his eyes. He wore glasses, one of which was painted an opaque white. When he took them off, you could see that the eye beneath the painted glass was clouded over. He could see out of the other eye, but not well enough to get around. Legally, as well as for all practical purposes, he was blind. When he came to live with us, he took my room, to which Mama objected strenuously but in vain. For Dad, it was a matter of respect to give the better available room to his father. But what got to Mama most was that Pap, as we called him, had not had indoor plumbing in Baltimore and was used to using what he called a slop bucket in his room and then emptying it out in the outhouse. In our house he used a bucket in his room and took it to the bathroom.

Mama, with her mania for cleaning everything top to bottom, was mortified. Pap was also used to having women as subordinates in his life, and Mama was a woman. A quiet war erupted between the two of them. It's easy enough for me to see now that I should have been Mama's ally, that she should have been able to talk with me easily, but I had already grown apart from her in so many ways that our conversations, instead of deepening, had become more and more guarded. I was fully absorbed in discovering who I was and had yet to take responsibility for even that process.

Pap liked to tell Bible stories, often to me, dramatizing them as he sat in our small kitchen. More often than not the stories were in response to some casual comment on my part or Mama's. An offhand remark about a bit of bad luck would prompt the entire story of how Job suffered but did not curse his Lord. As Pap told them, the stories were vital and powerful. It was the language of the King James version of the Bible that was both powerful and beautiful. Also a little scary. I thought of Pap's Bible recitations as God's-gonna-get-ya! stories. My relationship with God at this point was, at best, tenuous. "My lost saints" had not gone away, nor were they completely lost. Somewhere along the way I came up with the idea that I already had the ability to be the perfect being that God intended, and therefore I never needed to ask Him for anything additional.

Pap's coming to New York took from me the larger room, which Mama had redecorated, and put me into a small, cramped space that had as its only advantage a door that closed securely. My dad made me a small bookcase, which I accepted grudgingly, but I wasn't happy with it.

Stuyvesant High School had everything wrong with it. It was an all-boys school, which I didn't know until after I arrived. Because I had liked the science teacher in junior high, I thought the emphasis on science would be all right. I didn't know the standards and couldn't imagine that I would have difficulty with them. Stuyvesant was in decrepit condition, tucked all the way downtown, nearly an hour's travel from Harlem. Friends were telling me how wonderful it was that I had made it into this wonderful school and how really smart I must be. I took a wait-and-see attitude.

The first year I attended Stuyvesant, I went from noon until five thirty. The time I would have had for a social life was completely taken up by my new school hours. Eric was free in the mornings, but that was when we did our homework, and there was gobs of homework.

In addition, things were seriously beginning to fall apart at home. Looking back, I can see that we were all trapped in our own unhappy circumstances. Pap didn't like living in his son's house. My father didn't want the burden that it placed on his relationship with Mama, and Mama just hated that it seemed as if her life was being put on hold while Dad dealt badly with the economics of survival.

I don't know that he could have done more, and I feel rotten for having blamed him for being poor, and even more rotten for not realizing that I was doing it.

I would dream of meeting someone, a boy or girl who would be a secret reader as I was, who would feel the same sense of being alone as I did, who would want to meet me and be my friend. Together we would not be ashamed of being bright or liking poetry. The kids at Stuyvesant were all bright, among the brightest in the city, but my growing shyness made it hard for me to make connections. I longed to have a school sweater, a school jacket, the symbols of belonging. They were out of the question as we struggled just to make ends meet.

What Mama usually cooked was food with lots of dumplings or rich, heavy stews. She would often have me help her make desserts: fruit rolled in pastry, wrapped in cloth, tied and boiled, then taken out of the cloth, topped with icing, and baked. Delicious. When we had the money, we'd have bloodwurst or knockwurst and sauerkraut or sausages with baked potatoes and cabbage. One day, when Mama had made macaroni and cheese, Pap said that he never ate cheese, and that cheese was for poor white trash. That really hurt Mama, and we spent hours thinking of recipes that included cheese and disguising it so Pap wouldn't know he was eating it.

My first year's grades at Stuyvesant were miserable, due partially to the fact that I never studied. I had never had to study before and didn't recognize the need at this time. Most of my spare time I spent reading in my room.

Sometimes there are landmarks along the way to doom and destruction, seemingly innocent paths along which we merrily tread, smiling as we go, into the pits of Deepest Hell. My path was the romp of the Brooklyn Dodgers through the National League. I don't know why I became so fanatical about the Dodgers that year. It seemed that when they won, somehow I won, too. My sister Viola once said that I was the poorest loser she had ever seen. I wasn't a poor loser. To me there were two possibilities: winning and nonexistence. If a team I was rooting for had a good chance of losing, I was upset. I've fought teammates who I thought didn't try hard enough. I hold lifetime grudges. In my first year at Stuyvesant I invested all my hopes and dreams in the Brooklyn Dodgers.

The team was awesome: Peewee Reese, George Shuba, Duke Snider, Don Newcombe, Jackie Robinson, Carl Furillo, Rex Barney, Ralph Branca, Gil Hodges, and Billy Cox. They tore through the hot days of summer, knocking over all comers, winning with daring and flair. Then came the collapse of September. They couldn't buy a crucial win. The Giants, in the meantime, were surging. As the regular season's close drew nearer and nearer, the Brooklyn lead grew more and more narrow. Then it was over, and the Giants had caught the Dodgers. The season, my whole life really, was down to one crucial game.

Enough. No need to put myself through that agony again. The Dodgers lost. Bobby Thomson hit a home run off Ralph Branca to win the National League pennant at a time when I needed the Dodgers to win in the worst way. Kids from the Bronx were cheering throughout the school. I went home dejected. Mama was dejected, too, but she tried to comfort me.

Our English teacher, Mr. Brant, had us writing short fiction as well as reading Dickens's *A Tale of Two Cities*. How I suffered through that book. Dickens would not say anything in two words if he could substitute two hundred. But I loved writing short stories in Mr. Brant's class, and when we were assigned to write a longer piece, the class seemed to like the adventure story I wrote about a beautiful French noble-woman trying to escape from France after the French Revolution. Naturally, I had her captured by a press gang and made to serve on a French ship until she was discovered to be a girl and then barely escaping with her life and . . . and . . . and . . . My class loved it.

I was also assigned to a speech therapy class in Stuyvesant but found that if I didn't attend, no one seemed to care. I didn't attend. Again, while others had great difficulty in understanding me, I couldn't hear myself mispronounce words.

The late-afternoon sessions at Stuyvesant added to my isolation. I didn't have the after-school time that was available with the morning schedule. On weekends I didn't have the money to do much of anything. I filled my time writing and reading — writing for my own amusement that year except for an essay contest run by *Life* magazine for "the book I would most like to see in Cinemascope." I selected a book I had just read, *The Old Man and the Sea*. I wasn't in love with the book — I thought it was overly dramatic — but I liked Hemingway's writing, and I thought the scenes of the sea would look good on a wide screen.

My brother Mickey went to Textiles High, and that school was coed. I hardly ever saw him, but once, on my way home from Stuyvesant, I ran into him coming from 125th Street. We were walking down Morningside Avenue when we heard a woman scream.

"He's got my purse! He's got my purse!" she yelled, pointing to a dark figure running toward 121st Street.

Mickey went after the guy without a

thought and caught him on 120th Street and Manhattan Avenue. A passing policeman recovered the purse and returned it to the woman. The boy was a member of a local and very notorious neighborhood gang.

We didn't have much in the way of gangs. There were a few fighting gangs that mostly just paraded about looking tough and maybe committing a few petty crimes like the purse snatching. Their usual weapons were sticks, short lengths of chain, and an occasional knife.

The school year finally ended, and I threw away my final report card resolving to do better the following year. At home things were getting worse. Eric and I still got along well, but I became nervous about our friendship. We were at an age to explore dating, or at least parties. And I knew that I would not be welcome, as a black, at many of the parties to which Eric would be invited. Racism existed as a backdrop to our relationship, and I did not want to experience the humiliation of being rejected because I was black. For the first time in my life I was faced with the notion that I would have to deal with the idea of race as a central part of my life.

My parents had not prepared me to face

the kind of racial issues that I was seeing. Mama, Native American on her father's side and German on her mother's, was sympathetic to the black cause. Her mother had been ostracized because she had married a Native American. She had heard stories about the horrors of slavery, which she passed on to me, and knew something about the slaughter of American Indians. When *The Lone Ranger* came to television, she would watch it just to see Jay Silverheels, the actor who played Tonto.

My dad's advice on race was very simple. "The white man won't give you anything, and the black man doesn't have anything to give you. If you want anything out of life, you have to get it for yourself."

This was Herbert Dean's counsel on race relations. Actually, getting and doing for oneself was his advice on everything. He talked constantly about having two lists. One list consisted of things you wanted, the other of things you were willing to work for. I don't think that, having being raised in a segregated Baltimore, he ever imagined I would need to learn interaction with whites, or to deal with being black in any but a defensive manner.

In truth, everything in my life in 1951 that was personal and had value was white. All the authors I studied, all the historical figures, with the exception of George Washington Carver, and all those figures I looked upon as having importance were white men. I didn't mind that they were men, or even white men. What I did mind was that being white seemed to play so important a part in the assigning of values. I knew that the vague thought I had had earlier, that goodness and intelligence could somehow lift a person above the idea of race, was wrong. I wondered where and how I would fit in to a society that basically didn't like me.

The Garment Center

I was fifteen, starting my junior year at Stuyvesant, and I was lost. I didn't know where I was going or even where I should have been going. The other boys in the school began the term talking about college. There was an excitement in the air, as some were applying to a program at Yale that allowed them to skip their senior year in high school. There was quite a lot of talk about jobs. Future engineers, physicists, doctors, all sat around me while we waited for the beginning of the annual "Beat Clinton" rally. We wouldn't beat DeWitt Clinton's football team, but the rally was fun. A new friend, Stuart Miller, wanted to run a sporting goods shop. I could only think of him as the best writer in the school.

"I can get you a part-time job, man," my cousin Joseph had promised once when we met at my aunt's house. "Come on down to my place."

"I have to get a job through the school," I lied. I knew Joseph worked in the garment center, pushing a hand truck through the busy streets.

"Well, if they can't get you anything, come on by my place."

He wrote down the name of the company he worked for in the garment district. His handwriting was crude, childish. I took the paper and put it in my pocket, intending to discard it as soon as I could.

The garment center was once one of the busiest places in New York City. Located largely on Seventh Avenue between 28th and 41st Streets, it was where America's clothing was made and assembled. Successive waves of immigrants filled its factories, working for little above minimum wage as they cut, sewed, and hustled the garments into trucks to carry across the country. Mama had sometimes worked in the garment center, and so did my sister Geraldine. Gerry had a good job as a color matcher in a button factory, mixing dyes to any color a retailer wanted to make his dresses distinctive.

There were indoor jobs in the garment center, and outdoor jobs. The indoor jobs were represented by every race under the sun. People who spoke little or no English, but who could do one of the many jobs associated with putting a garment together, flooded into the buildings each morning and out again each night. On the edge of the garment district was the fur district, where the pay was somewhat higher.

The outdoor jobs, the men hustling through the streets with huge racks of dresses, or pushing hand trucks taller than they were, were largely black. Later, in their turn, Puerto Ricans and other Hispanics would move into these outdoor jobs. No, I didn't want a part-time job in the garment center.

The junior and senior years at Stuyvesant were morning sessions, beginning around eight and ending at one without a lunch break. It was possible to work after school, and many of the needier kids did. I heard about kids working in private offices in the neighborhood or at one of the insurance companies on 23rd Street. There was a job placement center, part of the guidance counselor's office, I believe, and I planned to go there looking for a job.

Jobs were, by and large, a mystery to me. My dad spoke of "good" jobs in the post office or on the police force. My sister Viola was working at an electronics factory on Long Island. I didn't know what she was doing at the time, but I knew she had once assembled television sets. Her husband, Frank, made signs. He had helped to make the Chesterfield cigarette sign at the Polo Grounds. The "h" in the sign would light up when a player got a hit and an "e" would light up when an error was made.

My aunt Nancy, Joseph's mother, the large woman who had run a bakery on the Lower East Side, now had a marriage brokerage business. She brought immigrant women together with American men and helped them marry. This allowed the immigrant to apply for citizenship as the wife of a citizen. All this was done, of course, for a fee. She had once arranged for my cousin Sterling to marry a black woman from Brazil. The woman was young and beautiful and seemed nice, but when the marriage got into trouble — and with her speaking only Portuguese it didn't have much of a chance not to — she changed. Sterling started to roam and stay out nights. The girl — I can't remember her name — went to a root shop in East Harlem, bought a number of herbs and roots, cooked them up, and dropped his picture into the boiling mess. He became deathly ill and had to beg her forgiveness. She left for Brazil within a year, hopefully somewhat wiser and surely less rich than when she arrived.

I applied for a job at school and was told there were none available but was also given the address of the New York State employment service. At the grimy state offices on 54th Street I was given a referral to Friedsam Coats.

"It's in the garment center," the clerk at the counter said. "Do you think you can find it?"

At Friedsam I was told that I would be packing garments for shipments and, if I worked out, I would be taught how to use the ticketing machine to put the sizes and prices on garments. There were two other blacks on the job, a girl who packed with me and the shipping clerk who took stuff to the post office. The pay was just above minimum wage, which suited me fine. I could walk from Stuyvesant to the job and stop, if I had the time, at any one of a dozen used-book stores along Fourth Avenue.

What Stuyvesant did, and did very well, was to prepare students to continue their education. If you were in the upper quarter of the graduating class at Stuyvesant, you were virtually assured of being able to get into a highly ranked college. The only question was which highly ranked college you would attend.

But it was the early fifties, and options

for black students were limited. Some of the black kids gathered in the small soda shop across the street and discussed their options. Many colleges in the South did not accept black students. The brochures didn't state it as much, but that was the reality. Guidance counselors and teachers would quietly pull a student aside and say that William and Mary, for example, did not accept blacks, so there was no need for you to apply. Many of the Jews were also worried about being accepted in Southern schools, and rumors of quotas for Jews in some other schools were also a worry.

There were always the Negro schools, such as Howard, Hampton, Morehouse, and Spelman. What they offered was an essentially segregated learning environment that not only taught skills but also brought accomplished blacks together in a way that reinforced racial confidence. The idea of voluntary segregation went against every value I had been taught. What did being born black have to do with excellence? The idealism I still nurtured as a fifteen-year-old did not have a racial component. Was life really about what restrictions I could accept or avoid?

In thinking about what college I might apply to, I ran into another problem.

Stuyvesant High School was ideally suited to the student interested in science or math. I didn't have a clue about what I wanted to do with my life. When I was nine I briefly wanted to be a lawyer. I can't remember what gave me the notion or even if I really knew what a lawyer was. At a party I got into a conversation with an adult I didn't know. The man asked me what I wanted to be when I grew up. "I want to be a lawyer," I said.

"You can't be a lawyer," the man said. "You don't speak well enough. You're pretty bright, so maybe you could be a law clerk and help other lawyers."

That brief conversation not only ended my law career but placed my speech problems in the center of my consciousness. The black man, a family friend, probably thought he was doing me a favor by pointing out that I had a speech defect.

I knew in my heart that I would have some difficulties in life because of my speech problems, and I also knew that I wouldn't always be able to solve them by punching somebody out. But I didn't want to make my speech the focus of my life. If I couldn't speak well, I could still communicate by writing. If the words didn't come easily from my mouth, they would, I hoped, eventually come from my writing.

I never understood my speech problem. The words I spoke sounded clear to me. When a teacher or classmate asked me to say something more clearly, I didn't know what to do. Reading aloud in front of an audience was especially difficult for me. After a while I dreaded reading even a sports page to my friends. My stomach would tighten up, and I would become so nervous I could hardly read at all. On more than one occasion, if I had to read in front of a class, I simply memorized a passage and recited it.

In my mind I eliminated any job that might involve public speaking. Still, as an immature fifteen-year-old, I was being asked to make life-defining decisions. What college did I want to attend, and what did I want to do with the rest of my life?

The idea that creative writing could be anyone's *job* never entered my mind. Did the dude who wrote

She walks in beauty, like the night
Of cloudless climes and starry skies;
And all that's best of dark and bright
Meet in her aspect and her eyes:
Thus mellowed to that tender light
Which heaven to gaudy day denies.

— Lord Byron — just do it for the bucks? I didn't think so. What's more, I didn't know of any living person who made money as a writer. The few articles I had read dealing with writers spoke about how they had conceived their ideas, or what they were currently writing, never about money.

But even more important than picking an area of study, I desperately needed a way to continue my education. My family had no money to spend on anything but necessities. I sent away only for catalogs to schools that didn't charge for them. When the catalogs came, I would take them to my room and map out plans for four years of study. First, I would take all the basic courses; then I would specialize in English literature or philosophy. I kept the catalogs in my drawer and pulled them out to compare buildings in the photos, trying to decide if I wanted to go to a school with modern buildings or if I preferred a more traditional building.

My reality was that it was more and more difficult for my parents to clothe and feed me in high school. Even with my part-time job I didn't have clothes to change on a regular basis or money for sports equipment. A coach who had seen me run asked me to come out for the track team. I wanted to do that, but I didn't have money for track shoes or sweats, and I was ashamed to admit it. There was no way I was going to show up, and I knew it even as I said I would be there. If I couldn't afford sweats and shoes to try out for a track team, it was obvious that I wouldn't be able to afford to go to college — not even City College. I heard about full scholarships, but they seemed few and far between. To me, not going to college meant that I would join the army of black laborers sweating and grunting their way through midtown New York. It also meant giving up all those values that I had been taught would make me a worthwhile person.

At fifteen I was interested in girls but considered myself too geeky to even approach one. My height, which was now slightly over six feet, had become a handicap in my mind. Instead of feeling tall, I felt merely incapable of not being seen. I didn't have the money for dating anyway.

Mama was struggling too. The numbers, the equivalent of today's lottery, were the dreams of Harlem and Mama's only hope to do more with the little money Dad gave her each week. In Harlem hundreds of poor people invested their pennies, nickels, and sometimes dollars in the hope that they would hit it big. A nickel hit paid twenty-seven dollars, half of the month's rent. A dollar hit was worth two months of hard work. Mama sometimes hit for two or three cents and sometimes for a nickel, but rarely did she make a larger hit. Still, every morning she would examine *Ching Chow*, a daily cartoon that supposedly gave lucky numbers. Any dream would bring out the Black Cat dream book for an interpretation and the accompanying lucky number. But even the occasional hit would mean, at best, a minor respite from the daily grind of barely making ends meet. Pap's medical bills added to the burden. We were never hungry or threatened with eviction, because when things got really bad, Dad could go down to the docks after he finished his regular job and work the night shift for a week or so.

I was notified that I had won a year's subscription to *Life* magazine as a result of the essay I had written on the book I would most like to see in Cinemascope. It felt good to be acknowledged for my writing talent outside school. Mama was happy for me, and Dad, as usual, didn't acknowledge it.

An event at my part-time job seemed to emphasize my predicament. One day when

I arrived at work, I found they had hired a white kid to work after school. He would take my place packing, I was told, and would learn the ticketing machine.

"You're a big, strong kid," the boss said. "You can start on the hand truck."

What he meant was that I could become one of the bodies pushing packages through the streets of the garment center. The boss dismissed my protests with a wave of the hand.

It was a done deal. The black shipping clerk loaded the hand cart that I would be pushing through the streets of the garment center. This meant to me that the white boy was being given the ticketing job because that's what they saw when they looked at him. They saw me as just another one of the hundreds of blacks who were fit only for manual labor. I told the boss I didn't want to take the cart to the post office. He said I would, or I wouldn't have a job. The black shipping clerk looked away from me as he stammered something about the trip to the post office not really being so bad. What I really wanted to do was to hit the boss, and, I think, the shipping clerk understood that. He found an excuse to step between us, and I turned away. I walked out feeling small inside, and very much ashamed that I couldn't have been more articulate about how I felt.

Hurt, I buried myself in my reading. One book, *The Gay Genius*, by Lin Yutang, told the story of Su Tung Po, the Chinese poet, artist, philosopher, and civil servant. What attracted me especially to the book was that the poet rose through the ranks of civil servant by taking tests and was appreciated as a poet at the same time that he was a civil servant. Race was taken out of the equation. It seemed a civilized way of conducting one's life.

I needed to work and found another job. L. Einstein & Co. sold costume jewelry, and I worked there through the Christmas holidays and into the spring. I wrapped, logged, and put the postage on packages of jewelry, which went to stores throughout the country. I read *The Foxes of Harrow*, a novel by Frank Yerby (at the time I didn't know he was black) and *The Well of Loneliness*, a novel given me by a shopkeeper on Fourth Avenue. I wasn't sure exactly what was going on with the sex in either book, but the conflict and longing between the women in *The Well of Loneliness* were interesting.

My response to my problems was to immerse myself in literature. Books are often touted by librarians as vehicles to carry you far away. I most often saw them as a way of hiding one self inside the other. What I had to hide was the self who was a reader, who loved poetry. This self was not the real me but was a very important part of the real me. And this was an idea that people around me could not seem to easily accept. People wanted to look at me and make a quick and simple decision as to who I was. I was big and I played ball and I fought, and those qualities meant, to a lot of people, that I must have a very limited intellectual life. Others were satisfied to label me as a black person and attach to the label any definition they might have as to what that meant. There were those who accepted me as a reader but then would separate me, in their thinking, from anything they accepted as black. But my life was filled with the cultural substance of blackness. I lived in a Harlem I truly loved. I went to church there, and grew up in the richness of Harlem's colors and smells and the seductive rhythms of its energy. Books, on the other hand, provided a dialog between me and the authors who had written them. They spoke to me, and I responded, not in words but in appreciation and consideration of their thoughts. More and more, I would respond with my own writing.

Buying a typewriter was part of the process. It was easy for me to imagine myself hunched over a keyboard, pounding out reams of deathless, hard-boiled prose. I made fourteen dollars each week in my part-time job and planned accordingly. Each week I gave five dollars to Mama for the household, I used four dollars for lunch, school supplies, and transportation, and the remaining five dollars also went to Mama to save until I accumulated the forty-five dollars I needed for the typewriter.

Working for the typewriter got my mind off college. When Eric called the house to ask if I wanted to do something on the weekends, I would say no, that I had to work to get the typewriter. Eric and I still talked from time to time, but things were difficult between us. In April 1952, by my calculations I had enough money to buy the typewriter and asked Mama for the money. She didn't have it. She had lost it chasing the numbers. I was crushed.

When my dad found out what had happened, he was angry. Mama's betting on the numbers, her chasing dreams, was out of control, and he knew it. She was also growing more and more depressed. She told me that she couldn't see a future for herself. Dad was working as hard as he could, but as in many black families, life had ground down to a bitter struggle for survival. Mama was also drinking heavily. I was filled with the bitterness of not having the typewriter for which I had worked so hard.

Dad decided to take on the task of buying me a typewriter. He went to his job and asked a secretary what kind of machine he should buy. She helped him find an old office-model Royal in a pawnshop. It had glass sides and looked as if it might have been used to write memos during the Civil War. When he brought it home and put it on the kitchen table, I wouldn't touch it. It was not the machine I imagined, or the machine I had worked so hard for. For the next months I hardly spoke to Mama, or she to me. I think that her hurting me made her feel worse than I felt. She began drinking even more.

It was almost May before I finally took the typewriter my father had bought for me into my tiny room. I wrote columns of I hate this typewriter and posted them on my walls.

I was doing badly in school, as I had expected I would, and so I stopped going. The school sent notes home, and I answered them by writing excuses on the unwanted typewriter and signing my mother's name to them.

God and Dylan Thomas

"How old are you?" The guidance counselor had put on her stern voice.

"Fifteen."

"Fifteen? Fifteen?" She acted as if she were surprised that someone that old still needed to be called to Stuyvesant's guidance office. "At fifteen you should know that you need to be responsible for what you are doing in school. Do you want to transfer?"

"No," I answered, subdued.

"Then you will have to get yourself on the stick, Mr. Myers. And you had better do so fairly quickly. I expect you to be in school every day for the rest of the year and on time, young man."

"Yes, ma'am."

"What do you do with yourself all day?"

"Nothing," I said, surprised that her voice had softened somewhat. "Nothing."

I had been out of school three weeks, leaving home each morning and walking to the subway, sometimes fully intending to go to school, only to get off the A train time and time again at 59th Street and wander into Central Park. I had discovered the pleasure of comparing different translations of the same work and would search them out. It was fascinating to me to see the small changes in language and phrasing from one book to the next.

"What do you do with yourself all day?"

Sometimes, if I had the money, I would go to the movies on 42nd Street. The Apollo Theater, the one on 42nd Street, showed foreign movies. I saw a film of Gorky's *The Lower Depths* there, and fell in love with Greta Garbo in *Camille*.

"What do you do with yourself all day?"

Sometimes I would go to Riverside Drive and look out blindly over the dreary Hudson River. I would take my notebook and write dark poems, which I would often later discard. They always said too much about me, and then again, never quite enough.

"So, young man," the counselor had said, putting on her the-interview-is-over voice, "I expect quite a lot of improvement from you. You have this end term and one more year to get yourself together and go on to college. Now report back to your homeroom teacher first and then your class."

I nodded, gathered my books, and walked out of the school. Years later I saw a movie, *Ferris Bueller's Day Off*, in which Ferris, the hero, was happily defiant and disdainful of the system. Everyone in his school was a cut below Ferris, as were his parents. His day away from school, replete with all the money he needed to enjoy the romp with his friends, was one of triumph. I didn't want to be defiant. I wanted to be in the system that I was walking away from, but I didn't know how to get in.

The school sent the end-of-the-year report card, and I read it, surprised that I had passed some classes I had rarely attended. They were looking for a way to pass me, and if I had passed the end terms, they moved me on. I resolved to do better the next year. Again.

Summer. The *Amsterdam News* assessed the chances of the Brooklyn Dodgers. If they lost again, it would be a blow to the chances of blacks in the major leagues, they said. The Dodgers had more black players than anyone, and the Yankees had very few. The Yankees were a white team. I had lost faith in the Dodgers' ability to win a World Series, but I still loved them.

I played little ball during the summer. There was a coaches' tournament up at

City College that I did get into, but my growing depression was affecting my game. I didn't believe in myself anymore.

I was thin, weighed less than 175 pounds, and fast enough to play guard, but the guys in the tournament were good. Some players came up from Philadelphia. Wilt Chamberlain was one of them. Ballplayers knew where the important games were going to be held, and the best ballplayers from all over the city were at the games. Coaches or scouts from around the country also attended. There were a few professional black basketball players in the National Basketball League, but not that many. The big push was to find players who might play college ball. I watched, mostly from the sidelines, and got into one game briefly, only to discover that the players were a whole level better than me. I got caught in a blind switch and found myself standing behind Chamberlain. He backed into me, and I felt his butt in my chest. I grabbed him when the ball came into the paint, and he went up as if he hadn't even noticed me hanging on.

There was a lot of talk about basketball scholarships, and I thought about trying to get up my interest in ball again. I played more that summer than I had for a while and began to see weaknesses in my game. Or perhaps it was just that whenever I looked at myself, I saw weaknesses where a few years earlier I had seen strengths. Fatty, my basketball coach, told me that my first step to the basket was good but that my second was weak.

"Your first step has to get you into position to get past the defender," he said. "The second step has to be strong enough to prevent him from recovering."

I went to the playground every morning to practice that second step.

On my way to one of these practice sessions I saw Frank for the first time. It was early morning, and the park was still empty of the hordes of kids who filled it each day. I was headed toward the first court when I saw a fight at the far end of the courts. There were three guys circling one. They took turns swinging at the guy in the middle, who was clearly not a good fighter. I went closer. One of the attackers had a chain, and the other two were using fists. They were all about my age, maybe a year or so older.

The fight wasn't my business, but somehow I was drawn to it. I moved very close to them, getting into their space, and was told to get lost before I got my face broken. I hit the guy who spoke to me, the one with the chain. His knees buckled, and he went down. The fellow being attacked, given a moment's respite, fiercely attacked one of the others. In a moment the three attackers were running toward the fence surrounding the basketball courts and climbing over it. They stopped long enough to issue threats from where they stood on the grass surrounding the basketball courts. Then they moved on.

The guy who had been attacked thanked me, and I asked him what the fight had been about.

He was six feet, with light, mottled skin and sandy brown hair with a streak of even lighter hair near the front. His eyes were large and pink rimmed.

He told me that the guys had wanted to rob him and had started the fight when they found out he didn't have any money.

He told me that his name was Frank Hall, and I told him mine. We walked out of the park together, and he thanked me again for helping him out.

"You don't mind fighting?" he asked.

I shrugged. No, I didn't like fighting, I thought. But something inside me was happy about being in the fight. It hadn't mattered so much that it was three against one, or that one of Frank's attackers had used a chain. It was more a feeling that, when I was fighting, I stopped feeling the sense of helplessness that seemed to be overtaking me. I had hoped to become part of a special way of life. That life would have had to do with ideas and people who took those ideas and shaped them into a kind of power. But that life seemed, in my growing isolation, ever more remote. It was as if I were standing on the sidewalk on the main drag of my existence, looking through the glass at all of life's goodies, but could not find an open door. Smashing the window would not make me welcome, but it would say that I was there.

Frank offered me half of the money he did have, and I refused it. He told me he lived near 116th Street. I didn't make much of the fact that he didn't give me an exact address. We said good-bye in front of my house.

At home two women friends of my mother's sat with her in the kitchen. Miss Dailey and Louise were drinking beer. Mama's speech was slurred as she told me to say hello to Jean, Louise's grand-daughter, who was in the living room. I went to the living room, said hello to Jean, who was about my age and thoroughly unlikable, and went to my room. In my room I lay across the bed and listened to the radio. I thought about what had happened in the park and knew that I liked hitting the guy who had the chain.

I also thought about Jean. I didn't like her, but she was a girl, and girls interested me. When I heard older guys talk about girls and sex, I was more taken with the way they talked about it than with what they said. They talked as if sex were the greatest thing that had ever happened and that it was normal to have sex foremost in your mind. I hadn't had sex, didn't know a thing about it except what I had learned from Eric (or thought I had learned), but I knew I didn't have the same degree of interest that was being expressed by some of the guys around the edge of the basketball court. Although I didn't know the ins and outs of sexuality, I did understand that there was a connection between homosexuality and being called "faggot." Faggots were often pictured, especially in the black community, as speaking with exaggerated precision, reciting poetry, and listening to classical music. Logically, I knew that loving books and writing did not make me homosexual, but more and more I hid those interests.

The church was the center of my community when I was a child, and much of who I was came from what I had been taught at the Church of the Master. What I understood, my philosophy, was based on the New Testament. I believed in this great sense of fairness, overseen by God Himself, that would reward the good and the pure of heart. But now things weren't turning out in the way I thought they should, and I didn't know what to do about it. I wondered if God was truly on the watch or whether religion, as well as my belief in God, would turn into yet another disappointment. I wrote a long letter to Reverend Robinson expressing my doubts. Two weeks later I received a letter from him that said, in effect, that when he, too, sometimes had doubts, he relied on his faith to carry him through.

That wasn't what I wanted to know. I wanted him to give me a telephone number that I could use to call God directly and get the straight scoop. I wanted to hear a big voice on the phone say "Yea, verily, this is me, God. It's all good, my man, and will be ultracool in the end. Don't worry about it."

Over the summer I read a biography of the anarchist Emma Goldman. I liked the book because much of it took place in areas of New York with which I was familiar. I was particularly interested in Leon Czolgosz, a young man who had tried to join the anarchists but had been rejected by them. Goldman said that he was a troubled young man looking for a cause to join. When he was rejected by the New York anarchists, he tried to prove himself by killing President McKinley.

"I killed McKinley because I loved the people," he is quoted as saying. Like Czolgosz, I considered myself an outsider and longed to commit the heroic act that would make me "belong." It was the same reasoning that some friends of mine used when they joined gangs.

We had read *The Red Badge of Courage* in school, and over the summer I read and enjoyed a history of the Civil War by Bruce Catton. This was my first major encounter with historical nonfiction, and I found it fascinating.

I was still trying to figure out the business of race. Most of what I read and heard was negative. Blacks had been slaves. Blacks had been lynched. Blacks could not eat in this place or that. There was little positive published about blacks except in the black press. The *Amsterdam News* ran stories about Negroes who had made good, and about some who hadn't. A new beauty parlor opened; "Bumpy" Johnson, the dope dealer, lost an appeal; and Langston Hughes, described as "the poet," gave a party.

Walking with my brother along Seventh Avenue, I once saw a gathering around a brown-skinned man who was being interviewed by some white reporters. Mickey and I went over and found that the man was Langston Hughes. We listened to him talk. He sounded like any black man on the street. There was nothing extraordinary about him, nothing that lifted him out of the ordinary. His humor was gentle, thoughtful. I was disappointed. When I pictured the idea of "writer" in my mind, pictures from my schoolbooks came to mind, and Hughes did not fit that picture. What I didn't admit was that neither did I. It would be years before I would meet Hughes again, and even longer before I would understand what we had in common, what we suffered in common. I didn't tell him that I was a writer. I wish I had.

I also heard, for the first time, the poet Dylan Thomas on the radio. He read some of his poetry, including "In the White Giant's Thigh," and "It Was My Thirtieth

159

Year to Heaven." He was said to frequent The White Horse, a bar down on the West Side. I went down to the bar, wearing my blue sports jacket, which I thought made me look older. The bar was full of beer drinkers, all white and at least in their twenties, if not older. I ordered a Coke, but the bartender, who wasn't a bit fooled about my age, told me to leave. I asked a bearded man sitting at the bar if Dylan Thomas was there. He had been, the man said, and had already been carried out drunk.

The man who related the story seemed disgusted by Thomas, but the whole scene was exciting to me, and that the man who had written and recited his poetry had been carried out drunk was wonderfully romantic.

I wanted to do something wonderfully romantic, to fulfill my idea of what I thought a writer should be like. Dylan Thomas, with his high, ethereal voice and poetry that was, at times, incomprehensible, fulfilled that idea, whereas Hughes, writing about ordinary people and about a very mundane Harlem, did not fulfill that idea.

"What are you writing about?" a student asked me in Stuyvesant when I returned in

September, full of hope and resolve. "What are you trying to do with your poems?"

What I was trying was not to do anything. What I was trying was to be somebody I could recognize as having the values and interests that I had learned were good. I wanted to be the person who wrote poems that moved the hearts of wicked men and made beautiful women swoon at my feet. I wanted to be the person who wrote with such a passion that all people would turn away from injustice and embrace the Sermon on the Mount. I wanted to write my poems and read them in a bar filled with shiny-faced admirers and then fall drunk and be carried off to a movie star's bed.

When I reentered Stuyvesant in September, I approached school with my game face on. I was going to do it once and for all. My resolve lasted for three weeks before I started staying out of school again.

Marks on Paper

School was becoming a disaster. Simple formulas in chemistry eluded me. Math problems that I should have handled easily became mysteries. We were given quizzes early in the year, and I fumbled them all badly. Again I was sent to a guidance counselor and sat in a wooden chair while he made a recitation of my faults. He asked all the right questions as to what I wanted to get from Stuyvesant, and whether or not I appreciated the opportunities I was being given.

"And for a student with your grades your attendance is atrocious!" he concluded. And then, punctuating his sentence with a gathering up of the papers on his desk, he asked exactly what my problem was.

Can't you see that I don't like myself and for all the reasons you are saying? Can't you see that I am more disappointed with my life than you could ever be? Can't you see that this school is only interested in what it sees as its successes and I know I'm not one of them?

He concluded the conference with an admonition that I had better get my act together or I would be in really big trouble. Again I walked out of the office and out of the school.

If it hadn't been for English, I would have never returned to 15th Street. The teacher, a dark-haired, intense woman, also ran the Creative Writing workshop.

"If any of you want me to read what you are going to write," she announced at the first class, "you will be responsible for a reading list of my choice."

She interviewed each of us, the interviews taking no longer than ten minutes, asking what we were currently reading, what we had read the previous year, and what we thought of the books. She already had samples of our writing. She said that she liked my writing, and wrote down a list of four books she wanted me to read. They were: *Penguin Island*, by Anatole France; *Buddenbrooks*, by Thomas Mann; *Père Goriot*, by Honoré de Balzac; and *The Stranger*, by Albert Camus.

It was the fall of 1953, and at sixteen I was beginning my senior year in a near panic. Most of the kids at Stuyvesant were just waiting for acceptance letters or scholarship offers. The grades from the junior year had already been submitted, and many of the students knew what schools they would attend. Sometimes I lied about being accepted to some school, at other times I said I hadn't quite decided, and most of the time I avoided the question altogether by not going to school.

I had not ever fully made the connection between my reading and the writing process. From time to time I had made superficial attempts to identify with an author. This usually meant, when I was younger, copying an author's style. Later it would mean imagining myself to be that author. Now my English teacher was insisting that I explore the two worlds, that of the books I read and that of my writing, and examine them for common threads. The first book I read was *Penguin Island*.

I wanted to like this book because I wanted to like what my teacher recommended. *Penguin Island* is the story of an island inhabited by penguins who, in the mistaken belief that they are humans, are blessed by a nearly blind monk. Blessings are reserved only for people, and it is decided to change the penguins into people. Thus is created a virginal society on which

164

the author can wreak whatever literary havoc he chooses.

The incident that affected me most in the book was the eventual canonization of Oberosia, a rather wicked person during her life whose reputation grew after she died and was manipulated by historians until it had become completely reversed. She was made into a saint, and fragments of her bones were considered to be sacred relics.

I was having problems with my own religious beliefs and did not need this interpretation by France. Could my religious beliefs be based on such convoluted history? It was the wrong time in my life for the book, but the right time as well, because of the clarity with which the author approached his theme. The book was less about what I considered to be the classic story form — the interplay between characters at a point of crisis — than it was about a broad presentation of the author's point of view. I had not thought about writing, or books, in quite that way.

When I handed in my report about *Penguin Island*, my teacher gave me back a report pointing out all the weaknesses of the work and reminding me that I did not have to love every word in a book to appreciate it.

My reading prior to my senior year had been largely hit or miss. I still read gobs of comics and an increasing number of trashy novels that promised any amount of sex content. I read *God's Little Acre*, by Erskine Caldwell, or at least parts of it, once a month. I also found a tattered copy of *Nana* by Émile Zola, which might have been a masterpiece, but I was only interested in reading the "hot" parts, so if it was a masterpiece, I completely missed the other parts. I had never had a sustained period of reading really good books before. I borrowed Anatole France's *The Crime of Sylvestre Bonnard* from the George Bruce Branch and read that while I was reading *Buddenbrooks*. I had dropped out of school again, so there was plenty of time to do the reading in Central Park or in Riverside Park, where I sometimes hung out just above the 79th Street boat basin.

Buddenbrooks was an intimidating book. The prose was so precise, so clean. The story was so logically laid out, without the gimmicks of *Penguin Island*. But it was chiefly intimidating because I was comparing my own writing to Mann's. I had never thought of writing as a competitive effort, but on one level it had to be. Why should someone read my work when Mann was available? Why should someone read my work when all the classic works were available and all of them were better than anything that I could ever produce?

I wrote a long report saying why I liked *Buddenbrooks*, and came up with as clever a list of negatives as I could. I also looked up how old Thomas Mann had been when he wrote the book and saw that he had been past twenty, which made him old enough for me to disregard, at least partially. *Buddenbrooks* had taken me into a different world, a different environment from the one I knew about, and the conflict between art and the expectations of the business world had touched me deeply. The book was not about my world, however. It had nothing to do with Harlem or with anyone whom I personally knew. The realm of great literature was still far removed from who I was and reinforced the idea that I was at a crossroads in my life, with only the lesser path available to me. I knew I would always be able to read good books and was fairly sure that one day I would be able to find them on my own. I was less sure that I would ever be able to write a good book.

I next started two books, Balzac's *Père*

Goriot and *The Street*, by the black novelist Ann Petry. I bought Petry's book because I thought it might be sexy. I liked it, but it suffered in comparison to *Père Goriot*.

As I went along the adventure of reading books selected by my teacher, I began to write again, began to put my marks on paper in the hope of constructing a world in which I would be comfortable. Putting marks on paper is always only a part of the writing process. The other part is looking at those marks and applying the judgment needed to ensure that the narrative that flies by your mind's eye will be recognizable to an independent reader. At sixteen I wasn't always sure what I meant. I also did not know who my audience would be. Would I write for black people like the guys I played ball with? I didn't think so. Would I write for a white world that I thought might exist but had never really experienced? And if I did, would my writing be accepted?

In the fall of 1953 I wanted to write stories with secret meanings that would relate to people like me, no matter their color or position in life. The stories would be short journeys from the mythical point of my mind to some wildly satisfying and morally logical end. I also wanted to put down on paper the labyrinth of my own fears as well as a safe path through that labyrinth.

During this period my writings from day to day were nearly incomprehensible even hours after I had finished them. All the pieces were there, but the puzzle of fitting them together was escaping me. I sensed I was losing control of my writing. I began to read Balzac.

Where Anatole France's work had been about ideas and wit, and Thomas Mann had been about precision and the ordering of character and plot, Honoré de Balzac, to me, was all about character. The story is about a retired merchant, Père Goriot, who has raised two rotten, spoiled daughters, and who spends all of his remaining life supporting them in a lavish style that drains him of all his resources. The daughters are thankless and heartless. When their father dies, they don't even attend his funeral. But no matter how shabbily he is treated, Goriot goes on, living out the obsession of his life. Away from the book I imagined myself to be Goriot, toiling away just beyond the edges of a world he could not enter. I decided immediately that I wanted to write like Balzac.

I imagined myself writing longhand, an

old-fashioned dip pen stabbing furiously into a bottle of black ink and then scratching with amazing precision across sheets of white paper. It almost, but not quite, supplanted my image of myself banging out stories on the typewriter. The old Royal typewriter my father had bought me was saved, I believe, by the fact that I could type really fast and had difficulty in reading my own handwriting even when I wrote slowly.

French was a subject that I had great difficulty passing. It was not that language was particularly difficult for me, but it seemed that I could put the phrases together only if I composed them from my own imagination and did not respond to the questions on the essays. And the oral parts of the course, standing and speaking the language, completely eluded me.

"Can you hear what I am saying?" the red-haired French teacher would ask me, impatiently.

Yes, I could hear, but I couldn't say the words in French any more than I could say them in English. I wanted to learn French because I wanted to read Balzac's dialog in French. The rhythms of his dialog, even in the translation, sounded perfect to me. I was so taken by Balzac that, in my imagination, I gave him a typewriter so that we would have more in common.

Sometimes Frank Hall would come to my apartment. He told me how great it was. I found out he was sleeping in hallways or in Morningside Park. Mama took an instant dislike to him, I think because of his eyes. They were always wide, red rimmed, and staring. His sandy hair was discolored in patches to a grayish blond. He looked black and yet nonblack, calm yet on the edge of turmoil, vaguely dangerous. When I read, I conjured images of the characters, and Frank, with his lean and hungry look, reminded me of Cassius in *Julius Caesar*.

Mama didn't like the idea of me hanging out with Frank until the small hours of the morning. She asked me what we did, and I told her that we just talked, which was true. He would also drink beer or Half and Half, a cheap wine drink. If he got in the mood, he would sing songs his father had taught him. Frank was the only person I was hanging out with on a regular basis. Other than him it was just the books.

If I didn't have money to get downtown, I would often climb a tree in the park. I could sit there for hours reading, the world passing below pretending to be real, me above doing the same thing.

The idea of reading a number of good books in a row added something to the process. I had always had trouble doing nothing either physically or mentally. If there were spaces, I was compelled to fill them, and the books were doing that. They also shut out the rattling noise that filled my head with warnings and admonitions — all in the voice of a guidance counselor — about where I was headed. I was now spending clear days reading in Central Park and rainy days in the movies. When I came home each day, I would check the mail and intercept any letters from school, answering those that needed answering and discarding the others. This worked for a long time until, one morning, Mama knocked on my bedroom door.

I was already up and dressed and gathering my notebooks.

"I'll be out in a minute," I called through the door.

It was early fall, and the apartment was cold. Mama had put on the oven and opened the door to let the heat fill our small kitchen. I sat at one end of the table, where she had put a plate of toast. I saw that instead of her usual housecoat she was dressed.

"Are you going out?" I asked.

"I'm going to school with you this morning," she said flatly.

Oh. When had I been to school last? I tried to think. Surely not within the last few weeks. Somehow she had found out, and we were going down to Stuyvesant together to pay the piper. She wasn't screaming, there were no demands for explanation, just the idea that she was going with me. Fine.

We didn't speak as we boarded the crowded A train. She had never gone with me to Stuyvesant, and she was probably suspicious when we changed at 14th Street. The L train that went from 14th Street and Eighth Avenue across to First Avenue was an ancient, rattling affair filled, on that morning, with boys wearing red-and-blue Stuyvesant jackets with the familiar pegleg figure on the back. Mama still didn't speak, and I wondered what was going through her mind. I thought about not going, of letting her go in by herself, but then I would just have to deal with it later. We went to the office.

"Walter, how are you?" The guidance counselor I had spoken to earlier looked at me.

"Fine," I said, shrugging.

All the notes I had sent in were produced. Mama was amazed at how well I had forged her signature. No, I hadn't been ill, not at all. No, she hadn't known I had missed nearly thirty days of school. Mama was taken into an inner office for a private conference, and I was made to sit outside. Several teachers came into the guidance office on business. My English teacher was one of them. She looked at me.

"Are you in trouble?" she asked.

"I think so," I answered.

"Whatever happens," she whispered, "don't stop writing."

I waited and waited, and then the door opened and I was invited into the interior office. I was asked about the time I had had scarlet fever. Scarlet fever?

My bout with scarlet fever came the summer when I was eight, and I had all but forgotten it. I had been hospitalized for three weeks, most of it in a glass-walled cubicle in Williard Parker Hospital on the East Side. At the end of the three weeks, when I was cured of the fever, the doctors had recommended that I be put into a facility for disturbed children until my "nervousness" subsided. Mama had refused and brought me home. But what was that about now?

"Are you having problems?" asked a school administrator, wearing his look-how-calm-I-am expression.

I didn't answer. It was clear that Mama had told them about the scarlet fever incident and must have explained that I was a nervous child. Still, I had violated the rules of attendance and certainly the rules of Stuyvesant. Mama and I were asked to sit in the hallway. A secretary brought Mama some coffee. We didn't speak as we waited.

Finally we were asked in again. I could remain in the school if Mama and I agreed to put me under the supervision of a city agency. Mama asked if I would go along with it and I said yes. I was officially disturbed.

The Stranger

As part of the new attention being paid to me I had to report to someone at a city bureau for an interview. Here a stern-looking man with white hair looked over my record and then announced, gravely, that I was in trouble. He became annoyed when I smiled and informed me that my truancy was "no laughing matter." I knew that, of course, but what had struck me as funny was that every time I got into trouble, the first thing that happened was that someone would think it their official duty to inform me of the fact.

He told me that if I continued staying out of school, I would be eligible for a juvenile facility. There was, on the cluttered desk between us, a badge that added weight to his argument. He had me agree to a lot of obvious things, such as that I knew my situation was serious, and that I was aware that I wouldn't be given many more chances. I had been warned about my attendance during my junior year, but my records hadn't been turned over to a city agency at that time.

It was apparent that the man interviewing me took my reluctance to answer his questions as insolence. He asked me if I thought I was better than everybody else. I answered no, of course. What we never discussed was how desperately I wanted to hide my feelings from him, or how ashamed I was of my predicament. I listened as he told me how I should be living my life, what I should have been doing with my opportunities, and how ashamed I should have been for giving everyone so much trouble. I looked down at my shoes. Thoughts of suicide flickered through my mind.

By the time I left, my stomach was churning. I got the A train at Chambers Street and stood as it lurched up to 125th. I had my books with me and looked through one of them. The words didn't make any sense, as all I could hear was the last recitation of my sins.

That night I met Frank. I had promised Mama I would be home early, but I needed someone to talk to in a bad way. There was nothing Frank could do to help me, but I didn't know anyone else who could, either. We sat on the park bench across from my house as it grew dark.

By this time I knew Frank's story well. His father had been a vaudeville dancer and singer and had achieved quite a bit of success in the black entertainment outlets. Some blacks were able to cross over into the white markets in the forties if their talents were not too much connected with the blues or low-down black music. The singing Mills Brothers, the dancing Nicholas Brothers, and Fats Waller had all crossed over, establishing their popularity in both white and black venues. Frank's father had bought a house in a fairly exclusive neighborhood on Long Island, which is next to New York City. Most of the year he traveled throughout the United States and Europe while Frank and his mom stayed home. Things were good for them until the father died.

Neighbors who had been kind to the black family of a famous entertainer were less than kind to the widow. Frank was beaten up a lot by neighborhood kids who taunted him because he was black. His mother couldn't or wouldn't do much about the bullying, and Frank responded by staying in the house as much as possible. Things went from bad to very much worse in one horrible incident.

Frank and his mother were on a bus going from New York to Long Island. His mother had been drinking and was loud, and the bus driver decided to put them off the bus. Mrs. Hall refused to get off the bus, and the driver tried to push her off.

Frank didn't remember anything that had happened after that. His next memory was of waking up in a hospital, secured to a bed. Later he learned that he had stabbed the bus driver and two other passengers to death. He was locked away in Creedmore, a New York City mental institution, from the time he was thirteen. When he was sixteen, his mother was able to get him out. She sold the house and moved into an apartment, and they lived together for a while. Then there was another incident. He and his mother were at a party. There was an argument, and he passed out. This time there was one dead victim.

Frank's first three victims were white adults. The last victim was black and close to Frank's age. Frank was put away again, this time for three more years until his mother got him out again. He was released under the custody of a priest from St. Joseph's, which was why he was in the Morningside area.

What I saw of Frank was an extremely mild-mannered young man, even when he was drinking beer, which he did a lot. When he found out that I didn't drink, he said he would make sure that I never started, that it was a bad habit. When I asked him why he drank if it was so bad, he said it was because there was so much stuff that he didn't want to remember.

"And when you drink you don't remember it?"

"No, I still remember it," he said, laughing.

We both laughed. I think he wanted to remember the things he had done and that in a way, it was all that he had in his life.

He still saw his mom once in a while, but he didn't like seeing her anymore. She kept telling him not to be crazy and asking him what he was doing with his life. He didn't remember too much about his father, only the way he had heard his father sing sometimes when he came home and sang to his mother. The last song he had heard his father sing was "Blue Velvet." When he had drunk enough beer, Frank would sing the song his father had sung, in a baritone deeper than his normal voice, the alcohol slurring the words in the darkness of the park.

As the time drifted toward midnight, Mr. and Mrs. Dodson came along on the other side of the wide street. She stopped when she saw me sitting on the park bench, and crossed over. She asked me if I was all right, and I said yes. She asked me if I wanted to go across the street with her, and I said no. I realized that the Wicked Witch was just being kind. I wondered if Mama had told her anything about my situation. As she turned to leave, I felt good about her for the first time.

I told Frank what had happened and told him I had been warned about being sent to a juvenile facility. He said that if things got too bad, he and I could live together. Frank was trying to get a place of his own. A guy on 123rd Street had offered him a job. He was to go to the guy's house at nine and get a package to take downtown. Frank also described the guy as a "creep."

I volunteered to go with him, and we walked down to the apartment. It was in one of the brownstones. We were buzzed in and went into a dimly lit apartment. There were dirty dishes in the sink, and food from the garbage had spilled onto the floor. The smells of incense and sweat mingled with cooking odors from another apartment. The apartment consisted, as far as I could see, of two rooms. The other room was dark, but I sensed something was going on in it. There were a number of people in the room we were in. The man Frank had gone to meet, a stocky dude in his twenties with his hair conked, asked him who I was, and Frank said I was just a friend. The guy glanced at me and told Frank to have a seat. I had a knife, an Italian stiletto that I had bought on 42nd Street, and I touched the pocket it was in with my elbow to make sure it was there.

The guy was putting something in paper bags at the table. Frank and I talked quietly. I glanced at one of the men against the wall, and it looked as if he was skin-popping — shooting heroin under his skin. A lot of people thought you wouldn't get hooked if you skin-popped instead of injecting the drug directly into a vein. I didn't know one way or the other. There were two girls in the apartment, and I wondered if they were dopers too.

We sat there for nearly twenty minutes before Frank was given a package to take downtown. He was warned that if anything happened to the package, he would be in big trouble.

We took the package Frank was given to

an apartment downtown near Roosevelt Hospital. Frank offered me five dollars, which I think was half the money he had made for delivering the package, but I didn't take it. We bought some potato chips and ate them on the way uptown as the new day broke over Harlem.

When I got home Mama was upset. She tried talking tough to me, but I just went to my room and closed the door. I thought a lot about living with Frank. Frank didn't read, and we didn't have a lot to talk about except what was bothering us. On the other hand, I thought, if I had a place away from my parents, I would have a place to bring a girl if I ever lucked out and got one.

The last book on the class reading list from Stuyvesant was *The Stranger*, by Camus. In *The Stranger* the protagonist, Mersault, has a chance meeting with an Arab, a stranger, that results in Mersault's killing the man. In examining Mersault's life, the judges see his detachment and come to the conclusion that a man who is so detached from normal human feelings is more likely to kill. Mersault is found guilty of murder.

As I read the book, it came to me that I could understand Mersault's distancing himself from the murder and also the lack of understanding on the part of the judges examining him. Murder was an essentially evil act. But what would happen if you could separate yourself from the act? Would it still be evil? When Frank blacked out, and awakened to discover that he had killed his mother's attackers, he had also removed the evil from the murder. Or had he?

Another idea I found, or imagined I found, in *The Stranger* was the use of detachment as a resource. Camus had given his hero a life that was not livable in any normal way. How would he get on with loving people who fully expected him to share a range of emotions with which they were familiar and with which they were accustomed to dealing? Although the state's prosecutors are made to seem almost ridiculous in the book, weren't their judgments the same as those of the ordinary people the hero would face every day? But Camus gives his hero a way out, though not one that many people would choose. He allows him a random act of violence that removes him from the dilemma of his life. I wanted to write about this deliberate detachment, about what people could do if they could remove themselves from the emotions they were expected to have.

I had to go to Bellevue for testing. The tests were given by a man who looked, to me, like the Joker in the Batman comics. The tests lasted nearly all day. There were intelligence tests and tests I recognized as psychological.

Bellevue was a city hospital, huge in dimension and unbelievably depressing. The walls of the long corridor where I was sent might once have been green, but as I sat on a wooden bench, waiting for the Joker to call me in for the next test, they were grimy gray with patches where the paint had peeled off, serving as landmarks for the roaches that scurried on irregular routes from floor to ceiling. A friend once said that it was a perfect hospital because once you were there for fifteen minutes you didn't mind dying.

The tests complete, I was given the name of a Dr. Holiday and told that I must see her, at Bellevue, the following week.

I was confused. I had not, to my knowledge, been accused of committing a crime, and yet I was now involved in a system of tests and appointments. I began writing about the process of going from agency to agency, being categorized, being advised of my shortcomings, and having dire warnings sent my way. I recorded everything carefully, writing in minute detail. But as I dealt with what was happening to me by becoming more and more the detached observer, I was becoming Mersault, the character, and not Camus, the author.

Dr. Holiday

The pace of my writing increased. When I was spending lots of time in Central Park instead of going to school, I would read three or four books a week. When I started back to school again, I tried to limit my reading to two books a week, and I filled my time by writing furiously. I could not do the assigned homework. I could open the textbooks, I could read the assignments, but then I would be drawn back to my own writing or reading. There were more notebooks with stories, more sheets of paper from U.S. Radium, where my father worked, covered with poems, or short critiques of books or plays. I tried to connect the books I read: a biography of Friedrich Nietzsche with his *Thus Spake Zarathustra*, Arthur Koestler's *Darkness at Noon* with Karel Čapek, getting most of my connections from works of criticism, reviews, or casual mentions by my English teacher, who seemed to have read everything.

For a while I went to school every day,

but soon I began missing days again. When I did attend, the teachers knew that I wouldn't be able to answer most of their questions, so they rarely called on me. I felt bad about not going to school but relieved at not having to sit in the classes and listen to lectures I could barely understand or to the chatter of students who were worried about grade point averages and S.A.T. scores. There was no doubt, either, that they were better students than I was. I was very unhappy and wrote droopily sad poems about death and isolation that reflected the way I felt. In a way I was mourning for the self I thought I had been, and at the same time I was becoming absorbed in the self I had become. Mine was the humiliated consciousness, ashamed of its every face, its every nuance. I was smart, which had come to mean that I was cutting myself off from people whose interests reflected their not being smart. My sole interests were literature and philosophy, which made me a bad student at the school I had selected. What I wanted was to hide myself, to not show the ugliness I felt. I was big, over six feet tall, too large to hide, too gross in movement and posture not to be noticed.

On warm days, instead of going to

school, I would go to Central Park and spend the day reading. I began *A Portrait of the Artist as a Young Man*, by James Joyce. I instantly felt that I knew Stephen Daedalus. He was an interested observer of the life around him, as I felt I was. His mother was a source of great conflict to him, as was mine. Ultimately, he would have to turn from her, which I felt was terrible. I didn't know if I would have that much conviction.

Poor Mama. She didn't know what was going on with me, and couldn't have known in a hundred years. We were, in our separate ways, looking to establish our respective identities. I didn't ever know who she really was. Years later, after her death, my dad would talk of how strange she had sounded when he first met her. She had a Pennsylvania Dutch accent peppered with German expressions that he didn't understand and, typically, laughed at. That was his way. I think, through the lens of many years passed, that she had counted on the constant of always being able to love me. The one picture I had seen of her as a young woman showed her in a shimmering blue dress, her dark hair framing her face, a fragile grace holding her in the studio photographer's chair. I would have liked to have talked with her after she had had her picture taken. I would have liked to have sat across from her when Fats Waller, tinkling the keys of the piano seductively with his thick, powerful fingers, rolled his big eyes at her. What had she expected of life?

Mama, too, had given me my first reading voice. She had helped me to move past just understanding the letters that made up words, and had coaxed me into making the words my own so that they danced in my head even away from the printed page. Then, in my teen years, I had developed my own voices, one that was still the child, her child, but another voice that was intellectually sophisticated in ways she did not understand. If I had told her that I had pain, she would have held me in her arms and comforted me. But to tell her that it pained me to question the meaning of morality would have, I think, puzzled her. I had not put away childish things, but neither were my understanding or my words only those of a child.

Stephen Daedalus did not grant his mother's request to pray with her before her death. Mersault moved away from the death of his mother. Mama was my key to life. Long before my father could or should have shown me the way to become a man, she had held me in her arms in silent definition of what it meant to be human.

During the summer I had gone to the Apollo to see Duke Ellington and Billie Holiday. Ellington's band was immediate, smooth, and magical. Billie Holiday came on at the end of the program to a wildly enthusiastic audience. She missed her first singing cue, then slurred her words in a whiskey vibrato. Someone in the audience yelled that she needed another shot of heroin. Somehow Ellington got her through a couple of numbers before she was hustled off the stage. There was an ugliness about Billie on the stage that filled the entire theater and lingered long after she had left. What had she expected from life?

To get to Dr. Holiday's office, I had to walk down a long gray corridor that seemed buried deep in the bowels of the hospital. I knew that if I had not scored so highly on the I.Q. tests, I would have been considered just bad, or rebellious. But I was certifiably bright and, therefore, disturbed. There were benches along the walls outside the doors with their frosted glass and their neatly printed names and titles.

"Are you angry about something, Walter?"

"No," I answered, truthfully.

"What kinds of problems are you having?"

I shrugged.

"Sometimes it's hard being sixteen, isn't it?"

I didn't know. I had never been sixteen before, and I didn't know what other kids were doing about it. Was there something about sixteen that was different?

Dr. Holiday was a beautiful black woman with a very pleasant scent. I didn't tell her that, even when she mentioned that, according to the tests I had taken, I seemed to have some difficulty in seeing colors. I wanted to tell her that I did have some small difficulty in distinguishing colors, but that I could detect odors very well. That, along with the fact that I could push up on the end of my nose and make oil pop out of my pores, was just one of my special talents. She told me how bright I was. Thank you. She told me what a good school Stuyvesant was. Thank you. She told me that the clinic was a place in which I could talk about anything I wanted to and at any time. She was confused about my name. She kept calling me Walter Dean when my name was Walter Myers. Hello!

After a long talk in which I tried my best to be as smart as she wanted me to be, she told me to come back the following week at the same time. I was not to forget the appointment or that I had made a deal with the school and with the city. When I came out of Dr. Holiday's office into the corridor, there was a thin black girl sitting on one of the wooden benches, her legs more twined around each other than crossed, her head in her hands. I wondered how I had looked on my side of the wall.

Home. Mama asked me if I had gone to the agency and I said yes. She asked me how it had gone and I said all right. She didn't know what else to ask.

That night I started my homework and quickly put it aside. I had picked up a copy of *Ulysses*, by James Joyce, and I started that. I read until midnight, stopping only to eat some spaghetti Mama had made. I had stopped eating meat, questioning the right of men to kill and eat animals, and so she had made the meatless sauce separate from the pasta sauce she and my father had, just for me. I had heard that *Ulysses* was difficult reading, and I wanted very badly to be able to read and love it; but by the time I turned out the light, I knew it was beyond me. I felt that Joyce had let me down, even as God had.

The newspapers were full of stories about the Rosenbergs. Ethel and Julius

Rosenberg had been executed the previous June, accused of spying for the Soviet Union. In a very real way I imagined my own execution. It would be the day of my graduation or, at least, the day on which I was supposed to graduate. I went to school only sporadically now, and was falling further and further behind. When the day came that my class graduated and, for the most part, moved on to college, I would be turned out into the world. But my being turned out would not be like Mersault's, stumbling toward his own execution. Mine would be the death of the Arab, senseless, anonymous, recorded only by the official records.

I ran into the gang that had attacked Frank in the park. I was reading in Central Park, at the sailboat lake, when four of them came along. One of them recognized me and called out to the others. They were out of their neighborhood, and weren't nearly as confident as they would have been if they had been in Harlem. One of them produced a knife, and I took mine out, flicked it open, and went straight toward him. Several white people started moving away from the benches. The kid with the knife, my age or younger, quickly backed off. One of the others told me to stay where I was while they went to get a gun. Sure.

The gang thing scared me. I didn't mind at all hurting people. That was the one thing I had in common with them, and they understood that. But that wasn't the life I wanted to lead. It was no better than being condemned to the garment-center labor force. Sooner or later, I knew, I would have it out with either all of the gang or some of them. On the way home I imagined myself facing them, blacking out, and waking to find that I had killed them all.

My next session with Dr. Holiday went well. She asked me about my family life and asked me if I had ever had sex with a girl. I answered that I had. I knew the answer I was supposed to give. I was black and sixteen. If what I had heard from other kids my age was true, they were all having sex. Then, just before I left, she asked a final question.

"Do you like being black?"

Being Black

It was a confrontation that I had not expected. Did I like being black? Dr. Holiday was a young black woman. Would a white psychologist have asked the same question so forthrightly?

"Yes," I answered. "Of course I do."

She accepted my reply without question. What else could I have answered? But the truth of the matter was that I really did not know what being "black" meant. When, as a young boy, I had been asked what I wanted to be when I grew up, I had never answered "black" or "Negro" or even "colored." I had answered "lawyer" for a while and, when I liked my science teacher, Mr. Marcus, I had answered "scientist." Later I had even considered offering "philosopher."

As a teenager I felt it was important to define who I was. I was a thinking being, and I wanted to know where I fit into the world. Even if the importance of defining myself had somehow eluded me, there were people around me who would not let me forget the importance of announcing to the world who I was or intended to be. I had taken interest tests in grammar school to indicate in what direction I should be thinking of going. Career advisors had asked me, at fifteen, about my intended major in college. From the time I was old enough to read, adults had asked me what I wanted to be when I grew up.

What did all the definitions really mean? How could I know what I wanted to be as an adult when I had never been an adult and did not know any adults who were doing anything I wanted to do? I was a male and did not know what that meant other than in terms of anatomy. But these two definitions, career and maleness, were a lot clearer to me than the idea of race. Someday I would have to make a living, so I needed some kind of career. I had a penis, and therefore I had to figure out what being male meant. The confusion in my mind existed because I heard, read, and saw different definitions of both career and maleness. In my Harlem community, career was defined as having a "good" job versus what my dad called "bull" work. I understood that by "bull" work he meant jobs that took little more than brute strength to perform. To me, this meant working in the garment center or its equivalent. It also meant my father's janitor job.

At Stuyvesant, career meant something entirely different. For most of my classmates it meant choosing a branch of science that they somehow knew about and would pursue. It meant choosing a major in college, getting grades, passing tests, and knowing where you wanted to go.

Being a man also seemed to mean something different in Harlem from what it meant in the rest of the world. I understood being a man as having some kind of power. In Harlem that power was expressed in muscle, in being someone who wouldn't take any nonsense or who was good at athletics. It was also defined as someone who had a lot of money or at least the trappings of money: a big car, an expensive watch, or expensive clothes. There was a sexual component as well. A real man paid a lot of attention to women.

I didn't see anybody talking about being a poet, or a short-story writer, as a career. Nor did I see anybody defining a real man as somebody who paid a lot of attention to books.

But it seemed to me that both of these concepts, career and maleness, were only subdivisions of the larger idea of race.

When I thought of the major careers, I thought of whites, not blacks. When I thought of maleness, I thought of whites with political or economic power and blacks with muscle. My definition of a black man was, except for the rare instance, a man without an outstanding career, and a man who had to define his maleness by how muscular he was.

These definitions were reinforced everywhere I looked. The history of the United States had been offered to me as consisting of the accomplishments of white people, mostly men, and the enslavement of black people. The great statesmen, the great writers, the great composers, as taught in schools, were all white. I knew that my own ancestors had been slaves in Virginia. But was what happened so long ago to my great-great-grandparents going to define me?

I wasn't born with a hyphen linking me to Africa, any more than I was born with a desire to dribble a basketball or to write. These were interests that I worked on developing. These were activities I chose. Being Afro-American, or black, was being imposed on me by people who had their own ideas of what those terms meant.

In the Harlem home in which I was

raised, the binding forces were love and survival, not race. Herbert Dean looked forward to buying his own home one day and spoke of land in the South that his family had lost. When Pearl Harbor was attacked and the Second World War broke out, my family was properly outraged. We bought small American flags to hang in the window to show our patriotism. I remember that one year during the war, my dad was away in the Navy, and the trees were coming down after Christmas. Johnny Lightbourne and I found a discarded Christmas wreath consisting of a red fuzzy material wrapped around newspaper, which in turn was wrapped around a wire frame. Johnny and I unwrapped the fuzzy red material and discovered that the paper was printed in Japanese! We immediately took the paper and wreath to the police station, along with information as to what obviously subversive family had discarded the offending decoration. We were Americans.

I had certainly heard the epithet "nigger" by the time I was ten. But that kind of language was not, in my mind, ever uttered by anyone except those who were unique in their meanness. It wasn't until my friend Eric was invited to parties that I couldn't attend, because I was black, that the idea of being a "Negro" began to have real meaning to me. Later, when I began to see how blacks were used in the workplace, which colleges accepted blacks and which did not, I began to think about race in purely negative terms. Blacks were the ones who were lynched, blacks were the ones who were barred from hotels, who had to drink from dirty fountains, who had to look for signs that told them if their race was welcome.

I had never sat down and said, "Let me think about being black." But somehow all the language of race, the history of what it meant to be black in America, all the "niggers" and all the images of slaves, and all the stories about my people being lynched and beaten, and having to sit in the backs of buses, had piled up in the corners of my soul like so much debris that I had to carry around with me. Being black had become, at best, the absence of being white. The clearest thing I knew was that there was no advantage in being black.

My answer to the question of race was to reject my identity as a black and take another identity. I could not identify myself as white, or as any other race. I could identify myself as an intellectual, and this is what I did, telling myself over and over again what white teachers so often told me, that race didn't matter if you were bright. When I came to the painful realization that my family could hardly afford to keep me in high school, and that college was out of the question, I knew also that I had lost even this adopted identity.

"Do you like being black?" Dr. Holiday asked.

"Yes," I answered. "Of course I do."

1954

The year started in a panic. January began my last term at Stuyvesant, and I wanted desperately to make it important even as the other students were just as eager to say that the senior year was not at all significant. All their college applications had been sent in, and many had already been admitted to schools. Their grade point averages counted only for bragging rights. I was still hoping for a miracle.

The newspapers were already revving up for the coming baseball season. Black newspapers were claiming that the Negro Leagues were dead, and that seemed to be the case. I read about the Dodgers, how Jackie Robinson's legs were doing, and what Gil Hodges thought about the coming season. Sports were still attractive to me. You can love a baseball team without worrying about not being loved back, or about being awkward in your approach. Baseball teams will allow you to love them and to show emotion when people turn away from you. And when the team wins, when the team gets the needed hits and the runs flood across home plate, the love is returned, and there is satisfaction. I read about the Dodgers' chances, and that they looked strong. I hoped, but I didn't believe, not even in my beloved Dodgers.

The radical newspapers were full of stories about Vietnam. The war was clearly going badly for the French, and commentators were warning that the United States needed to avoid involvement.

Frank came to my apartment, and Mama was afraid of him. I showed Frank my room, and he was impressed with how many books I had. My small bookcase was jammed with books, and there were books in piles all over the small room. Frank told me that the same fellow on 123rd Street who had hired him to deliver a package had offered him money to beat up a junkie who owed him money. He said he had not made up his mind yet if he wanted to do it. I asked him to let me know.

"He looks so strange," Mama said after he left.

Frank looked the way I felt. He was an alien on this planet, and I was drawn to him for that reason. I wanted to think of myself as someone different. Different meant that you were not responsible for the normal things in life.

What I wanted to do was create a world to replace the one that I felt had failed me. I had spent fifteen years of my life trying to expand my universe because I had been told that was what I should do, but there was no breadth to my world, no experience that would tell me what to do now that I was in trouble. Dr. Holiday said that she wanted to help me see my strengths, but I thought I did see them. My growing understanding of literature was a strength, even if my intense interest in it isolated me from people around me. My ambition to make things right, to mediate between God and man to bring fairness and justice to the world, was a strength, even if it isolated me from the guys I played ball with. I thought that my seriousness was a strength, even as it isolated me from the teenagers around me who were busily discovering the importance of their own sexuality and how much fun their lives could be. I knew my strengths well, and they were killing me.

Although I wanted a miracle in school, and knew full well that the miracle should somehow involve academic study, in reality

I spent my time reading. I found a socialist bookstore and read a history of the labor movement. There was a week of reading François Villon and not liking him at all. There was a week of reading Siegfried Sassoon's war poems and being deeply touched by them. It was not the language of Sassoon but the violence of war that attracted me. Wars, I believed, were fought for noble causes, and it was easy to imagine myself lying in the trenches, weighing my words against the pain of dying, thinking that death could be a satisfactory answer to failed promise. I imagined people asking whatever had happened to me. Did he simply fall by the wayside? Was all his brightness really just a charade, a pose he had affected before the spotlight fell upon him and revealed how much of a nothing he really was? Or did he simply become a Negro, sweating and straining through the streets of the garment center with all the other Negroes? Did he simply sit in the park, a book propped on his lap, pretending to read as the real world passed him by?

Surely, if the answer to the question was that I had died in some glorious adventure, I would have, at least, not failed.

At Dr. Holiday's office she asked me

what I had been thinking about during the week. I told her that I thought that dying in battle was not a bad thing. She called Mama and asked if I had ever tried to kill myself.

As spring approached and the end of the school year neared, my anxieties increased. Even the books I loved were becoming harder and harder for me to deal with. Stuyvesant was impossible. The successful members of the senior class were merely going through the motions. On one of my rare visits to school a teacher who'd taken an interest in me gave me a book by André Gide and asked what I had been reading. I was reading some poems of Gabriela Mistral and told her so.

"Are you writing?" she asked.

Yes, I was still writing, but the marks on paper made less and less sense to me. I was removed from the logic that had once made my stories and poems easily accessible. Now much of my writing contained remnants of too many thoughts and had too many obscure references. I was having difficulty understanding material I had written only days before.

There was another encounter with the gang that had attacked Frank in the park. About fifteen of them were walking down

121st Street when I suddenly found myself walking just yards from them. One of them recognized me, and they started to chase me down the street and onto Morningside Avenue. I was fast and moved away from them. Two of them caught up with me in the hallway of my building, and I fought them. One had a small length of chain, which he swung. I caught it and jerked it away from him and swung it myself. They backed off and ran outside to call the others. I ran up the stairs to the roof, and across the rooftops to a building on the corner.

Later that evening, lying on my bed, I thought about what had happened. I hated the gang thing with a passion. They were idiots intruding on my life, but, like the idiocy of racism, there seemed to be nothing that I could do about it. The gang exerted its power over its turf, and I was living on what the gang members considered their turf. It was what they valued, and they needed to deal with me. I imagined myself fighting them, inflicting far more violence on them than they ever could on me. I knew I could hurt any of them in a fight, but more than that I wanted to hurt them.

On the 17th of May the Supreme Court announced the decision to condemn the "separate but equal" philosophy of education. *Brown vs. Board of Education* had been won by the National Association for the Advancement of Colored People. Blacks were cautiously hopeful that this might be the end of segregation.

There were more letters to my house from school. I intercepted them and read them and even called the school to tell them why I wasn't coming. I told a counselor that Dr. Holiday wanted me to stay out for a few weeks to get myself together. They asked me to have Mama call and tell them that, and I told them that she would. Naturally I didn't tell Mama.

I knew I had to do something about school, that eventually there would be the phone call that would reveal how many weeks I hadn't attended, and I would be in trouble all over again. One day I got up my nerve to go to school and see what was going on. If there were a confrontation, I thought, I would assume my new persona of "disturbed" student and use it to bluff my way through.

On the A train I rehearsed my story in my head. I hoped I wouldn't see Eric or any of the other guys who had gone to junior high school with me. I had kept away from them as much as possible over the last year, and they didn't know what was going on with me. At 14th Street I almost chickened out again. It was not the trouble that I was in, or could be in — I didn't think they would send me to reform school even though that had been a threat — but I didn't want my humiliation put on public display.

It was a sunny day, and 15th Street was nearly empty. Usually there were one or two latecomers rushing to school a half hour late. I looked at my watch. The homeroom period would be over, but I was only fifteen minutes late for the first class. I tucked my books under my arm and went to the door and tried it. It was locked. I went to a second door. It was also locked.

"What are you looking for?" A voice behind me spoke.

I turned and saw a man in overalls, a paper cup of coffee in his hand, a ring of keys hanging from his belt.

"I go to this school," I said.

"Well, they're closed for the year," he said. "If you left clothes or books in there, you're going to have to wait until it opens in September to get them out."

It was over. Quite simply over. The school year had ended. The graduation exercises had been held, and the senior class of Stuyvesant High School had moved on with their lives.

"Oh," I said. "They'll be open in September?"

"Yeah, the regular time," came the suspicious answer.

I left, walking slowly uptown, crying. It was so far from what I wanted for my life.

Sweet Sixteen

I was sixteen and adrift. I had no ideas, no plans, and little hope. I didn't tell my parents what had happened. For the next week I got up each morning and left as if I were going to school, carrying my notebook and something to read in the park. I didn't read. I didn't write. The words on the pages had stopped making sense, and nothing I could write was adequate to express the despair I felt.

Eric called and left a message with Mama. He wanted to see me. I imagined his mother looking for me at the graduation ceremony, asking him where I was. I was too embarrassed to see him and didn't call back.

Things that had been so familiar just days before my last visit to Stuyvesant became strange, and I felt I was losing the mental faculty for making sense of the world around me. My father kept a careful distance between us. He didn't know me. My guess was that he didn't really think much of what I had become. One time, when I was leaving the house around midnight, he stopped me and asked me where I was going.

"Out," I said.

He told me to stay home. I said no, and walked out of the house. I spent the night walking through Central Park, not coming home until dawn.

Often I would lock myself in my room, and I could hear him asking Mama what I was doing. Mama would always give him some answer, and sometimes, loud enough for me to hear him, he would say that it wasn't right for anybody to stay in his room as much as I did. Mama would just tell him to leave me alone.

It was years before I discovered the shame that hid him from me. My father couldn't read. He had no idea how to reach the person I had become and was too embarrassed to let me know. When, a lifetime later, he lay, a fragile remainder of the powerful man he had been, in the veterans' hospital in East Orange, New Jersey, I brought him the only gift that had meaning to me, a book I had written. He looked at it and put it down on the white hospital table next to the bed and smiled. I wanted to beg him to pick it up and look at my words, to tell him that it was all I had and all I was. I think he knew, but there was nothing he could do about it. The printed words were a code that forever separated us.

Frank called. He had agreed to make another delivery and wanted to know if I wanted to come along.

I met Frank at the entrance to the park and asked him what was up. He didn't trust the man we thought was a dope dealer. He wondered what I thought of him doing the job. I thought he wanted me to talk him out of it, to say that it was too risky, but I wanted to do it.

As soon as we arrived at the apartment on 123rd Street, the man cursed Frank a lot, which angered me. Frank was quiet, taking the verbal abuse, looking down at his hands. We made the arrangements, and I was glad to get out of the filthy apartment again.

We were supposed to pick up a package from a man in the subway at 96th Street. He was white and would be wearing a blue blazer. Frank got five dollars with the promise of another five when he brought back the package. Outside, Frank asked me if it was still all right with me. Yes, it was.

We took the local down to 96th Street, and I told Frank to walk ahead. I would follow him. There weren't many passengers getting off at 96th and only a handful getting on. I knelt and fooled around with my shoelaces as the train left the station. There was a blond guy wearing a blue jacket. He didn't look like much, and I relaxed as Frank went up to him. The bathrooms in the subways were open in those days, and the guy nodded toward the men's room. Frank followed him in.

They were still in the bathroom when the next train came and left, and I wondered what was going on. When the train cleared the station, I went to the bathroom, opening the door as if I were just a casual user. Frank and the guy were in one of the booths, fighting. Frank was struggling, making whimpering noises as the other guy tried to pin him to the back of the booth.

I hit the guy in the back of the neck twice, and he slumped forward, sliding down Frank's body. I pulled Frank out of the booth, and we ran out of the bathroom.

"What happened?" I asked.

"He jumped me," Frank said. He was trembling and panting for breath.

We were almost to the exit when the guy came out of the bathroom. He had a gun in his hand. We jumped on the tracks and ran the distance from 96th Street to 86th, where we climbed up, rushed past a group of startled people waiting for the train, and made our way out of the station and into Central Park.

"He set us up," Frank said, his voice incredibly high. "He set us up!"

Frank went on about what he wanted to do to the guy. I knew that if Frank became upset enough, he could kill the guy, but he probably wouldn't reach that state. He would probably get beaten up himself, or maybe worse.

Frank's arm was raw from being scraped against the booth when he was struggling with the guy in the bathroom, and we put some water on it. Then we walked downtown to the Automat. We both had coffee and donuts.

"Did you like doing that?" Frank asked me.

No, I didn't. It was brutally physical, and ugly — although in some small way there was a sense of excitement to the incident in the subway, a sense of being, if not powerful, then less weak. And it was something I could somehow emotionally manage with ease. There was a danger, I instantly knew, that the feeling of power, even temporary, could possibly draw me in, could trap me the way that the temporary relief of drugs trapped people.

The garment center and fighting were connected in my mind, and I couldn't sort them out. I hadn't been nervous in the bathroom. I wasn't nervous until I got home that evening. I wrote down what happened, making it seem more an intellectual exercise than it was, then tearing the paper out of the machine and throwing it away. It had not been an intellectual exercise, no matter how I tried to push it in that direction. I was not walking down a beach and encountering a stranger. This was a possible reality, a kind of life that existed all around me. It was calling my name.

Frank had spoken of going to 123rd Street and killing the man he thought had set us up. He was trying to be as macho as he thought I was.

Dr. Holiday had said that nothing I told her would ever be repeated. When I told her what had happened in the subway, she was shocked and wanted details. I was instantly sorry I had told her anything. She asked me more questions about Frank. Did my mother know that he was my friend? Did I think I was going to be involved with this Frank person anymore? I honestly didn't know. I think she called my house, because Mama later asked me if I was in any trouble and was I still hanging around with Frank. I told her to stay out of my business. I didn't know what Dr. Holiday had found out about Frank, or what she had told Mama, but I knew that Mama was really upset for the next few days.

The French were losing the war in Vietnam, and the papers carried a story about a French nurse they called "The Angel of Dien Bien Phu" who had cared for French soldiers when that village fell to the Communist troops. I had read the dramatic poetry of Wilfred Owen, who had been killed in the first world war, and took to filling pages with my own romantic poetry about the nurse, war, and heroic deaths.

A week later Frank was beaten up badly by two men who had followed him in the park. They were older guys, so he assumed they were from 123rd Street. I was surprised. I thought that if someone really was beating him up, he would have killed them.

Frank wasn't supposed to leave New York City without permission, but he decided to go to Philadelphia, where he thought a friend of his father's might live. It was risky. He was still involved with the legal system and was always under the threat of being institutionalized again if somebody bothered to check on him. Also, he couldn't get his medication if he was in Philadelphia. It was better than being beaten up, though, and I went downtown with him to the Port Authority bus terminal on 42nd Street. He told me he would come back when things cooled down a little. If he got settled in Philadelphia, he said, he would send for me.

I had attached myself to Frank. I felt he was living on the edge of being out of control, of not being responsible for who he was or what he was. I also liked him. I liked sitting with him and hearing his stories of life with his father, even though I thought he had made a lot of it up. I liked hearing him sing sad songs in his gentle baritone voice. With Frank leaving, the world I had thought could not get worse was suddenly worse. I was being chased by the gang that had attacked him, and now I was worried about Frank and whoever it was who had beaten him up.

When Frank's bus left, I thought about walking home. I was tired, but lying down to sleep wouldn't help. It never did. Before leaving the bus terminal, I stopped at an army recruiting stand and asked how old you had to be to join the army.

"Eighteen," I was told. "Seventeen if you have your parents' permission."

"Suppose your parents are dead?"

The neatly dressed soldier shrugged and asked the noncom who worked with him. I was told that if your parents were dead, you could probably join the army at seventeen.

I was sixteen, but I would be seventeen on the twelfth of August.

I was at the recruiting office in the Bishop Building on 125th Street at nine o'clock on the morning of my birthday. I was seventeen and ready to join the army. There was an entrance test to pass. I took it, and the black sergeant said it was the highest score he had ever seen. He gave me an application, and I filled it out. He looked it over and asked me if I really wanted to be in the army. I said yes, and he tore up my application.

"You sign the form," he said. "I'll fill it out."

I signed the form and watched as he filled in the blanks. He handed me the form and told me to look it over. He had given me a squeaky-clean background, with dead parents, and had even taken out the fact that I had become a vegetarian. He told me to call him in three days. I did, and I found I had been accepted into the army. I would enter on the following Monday.

I waited until the weekend to tell my parents. Mama cried and asked me why. I didn't know what to say to her. I hadn't yet sorted out the shame I felt for having squandered my life, which, at seventeen, I thought was nearly over anyway. Nor was I, with all my reading and writing skills, articulate enough to express my sense of being lost. I didn't know enough about life or even about the ideals I was chasing to know what I was lost from. What I did know was that I wanted to get away from home, away from Harlem, away from anyone in the world who might care to ask what I would be doing with my life.

My dad said that it was a good thing that I had entered the army, that I would be all right there. I heard him say to Mama that it would make a man out of me. He wanted me to hear him say that, and I don't think he meant it in a bad way. He wanted to somehow reassure me that I could be a man, whatever that was supposed to mean.

I told my brother Mickey, and he wanted to join, too, but for some reason did not. My other half brothers, Buddy, Sonny, and Robert, asked me what being a soldier was like, and I made something up that sounded vaguely heroic.

On the day I left, Mama was up early, sitting at the place at the kitchen table where she always sat, the ashtray in front of her already half filled with partially smoked butts.

"Take care of yourself, boy," my father said. He gave me a New Testament that he had carried when he was in the Navy, and a money belt. It was what he had to give me.

Mama couldn't speak. We looked away from each other. I needed to be strong enough to walk away, to invent a new life for myself without her, and she needed to look inside herself to see what truth in her life had allowed her to lose her son. We looked away from each other, but I knew she was crying.

The early-morning station at 125th Street had the first of the army of black workers headed downtown to sort mail, to carry bags, to push racks through the busy New York streets. I had a small bag with an extra pair of pants, some underwear, an extra shirt, and a notebook. I took out the notebook and began to write as the train jerked its way out of the station, out of Harlem. I had just ended the first part of my life.

The Typist

As a child I wrote, but I never considered writing as a job or career. It would have been, I believe, considered sacrilegious for any of my early English teachers to mention that a Shakespeare, a Shelley, or a Keats even considered accepting money for the words. None of my acquaintances and no one in my family wrote, and yet I have become a professional writer. When I look at what seemed at first a highly improbable circumstance, it all seems so amazingly logical. I am doing what I should be doing.

To begin with, I have been an excellent reader for most of my life. Long before I knew the meanings of all the words I encountered, I was able to approach books with confidence. All those conversations with Mama in that sunny Harlem apartment, conversations meaningless to anyone but us, prepared me to use language in special ways, making it my own. This opened wide vistas of scenes and locales that I did not so much visit in my reading, but rather possessed. I *rode* on the back of the South Wind in search of the handsome prince. I *trembled* when I heard the voice of the Giant Troll under the bridge. The more I was able to absorb in this process, the more I wanted to absorb. I was like an archaeologist, in a state of constant discovery.

I found, stumbled upon, was led to, or was given great literature. Reading this literature, these books, led me to the canvas of my own humanity. Along the way I encountered values that I accepted, primarily those that reinforced my early religious and community mores. My reading ability led me to books, which led me to ideas, which led to more books and more ideas. The slow dance through the ideas led to writing.

I was also lucky. Lucky that I wasn't killed in my encounters as a teenager, or did not end up in jail. I left home on a Monday, the twentieth of August, 1954. Within days of my departure for the army the police were at my parents' apartment, looking for me.

The army. Numbing years. Years of learning to kill efficiently. Years of teaching others to kill efficiently. Years of nongrowing, from being a seventeen-year-old, smooth-faced idealist hunched over a book in his Harlem apartment, to becoming a smooth-faced veteran of twenty hunched over a beer in a post exchange.

All the poetry of war had left me upon my first scenting of decaying flesh. The atmosphere of non-thinking had been a godsend when it allowed me to forget my own failures as a teenager. It became a curse when it was all that I saw around me and before me. As glad as I was to have my entrance into the military rescue me from the dangers of the street, I was doubly glad to be released.

During the years following my army experience I found myself in a series of low-paying jobs. I worked in a factory in Morristown, New Jersey, where my parents had moved. I worked in a Wall Street mailroom and finally found a job in the post office from which I was fired because I could no longer stand the stultifying work. From the post office I found a job as an interoffice messenger just blocks from Stuyvesant High School.

I continued to read at a good pace, but I had all but given up on the writing. Then, one day, while I was on a construction job in midtown Manhattan, I found myself at low point in my life. I had spent the morning knocking down interior walls with a sledgehammer and was covered with dirt and debris as I ate my lunch on the curb. A fellow worker nudged me as a young, pretty girl passed. He made some remark, and I looked up in time to see the absolute disgust in her face. I knew this was not what I wanted to do with my life, and I remembered my high school writing teacher's advice: "Whatever you do, don't stop writing."

I decided, then and there, to start again. I didn't need to get published, or to make money from my writing; I just needed to be able to think of myself as a person with a brain as well as a body. I bought a composition book on the way home, and that night, after bathing, I began once again to make marks on paper.

It was refreshing to write again. It was as if I were suddenly back in my element, searching for the right words, hearing the music of language once again. My poetry was all vanity, the gathering around me of the accoutrements of an inner life. I would send my poems out, to literary quarterlies or magazines, and wait for their return. While they were out, I would dream of their appearing in the pages of some magazine, of a stranger musing over my words, of a phrase that I had written wandering through the mind of a subway rider. The poems almost always came back, and I would send them out again, asking no more than that by their absence they would offer the promise of immortality.

Once I began writing again, I couldn't stop. I produced poems, short stories, articles, even ideas for advertising campaigns. I would save my rejection slips, and every six months or so I would put them into a neat pile to check my progress. Then I would throw away the pile and start a new one. Eventually a few of the poems were published, and then a few of the stories, mostly in small literary magazines that paid in contributors' copies.

A turning point in my writing was the discovery of a short story by James Baldwin, "Sonny's Blues." It was a beautifully written story, but, more important, it was a story about the black urban experience. Baldwin, in writing and publishing that story, gave me permission to write about my own experiences. I was playing a lot of ball at the time, and my next story, about basketball, was accepted the first time I sent it out. When my half-brother Wayne was killed in Vietnam, I was able to handle the grief of his loss by writing about it for *Essence* magazine.

I found other black writers, in particular the journalist Chuck Stone, and I met John O. Killens, who in turn introduced me to James Baldwin. I tried to explain to Baldwin, who had grown up just blocks from me in Harlem, all that "Sonny's Blues" had meant to me, but I couldn't.

"It's a shame we all have to go through that process, isn't it?" Baldwin said knowingly.

Killens, the author of *Youngblood*, *And Then We Heard the Thunder*, and other novels, also brought me into the Harlem Writer's Guild, an organization of black writers. He counseled me always to think of my body of work rather than to concentrate too heavily on a particular book. It was, I believe, good advice.

In the interim, despite my lack of college, my reading skills had allowed me to get better jobs. I wasn't making a lot of money, but I realized that my ability to handle any written material gave me a versatility that many of my friends looking for jobs did not have.

I also began making some money from writing articles and fiction for men's magazines. It wasn't a lot of money, but it was enough for me to call myself a writer.

Then, in 1968, I entered a contest for black writers run by the Council on Interracial Books for Children. I won the contest, and the book was published the following season. I have been publishing books for young people ever since.

In putting together the memories for this book, lining them up and trying to make sense of them, I've come to the conclusion that I had a marvelous start in life. The love and attention I received as a toddler allowed me to acquire skills beyond those that my parents enjoyed, and in some ways to grow beyond the point at which my relationship with them was easily managed. I was fortunate to be raised in a church and community that gave me an appreciation of values that I have, from time to time, bent somewhat, but that have always brought me back to a core in which I am satisfied. It was in my childhood community that I was first exposed to the cultural substance that is so much a part of my writing today. Through those early years, the years of halted speech in which fists flew faster than words, I was able, with the love of my family, to claim ownership of the language I would spend my life enjoying.

In my heart I've always wanted to do the

right thing and be thought of as a good person. Even here I see that I've excluded many of the discipline problems I had in school. By today's standards I might have been described as hyperactive. I like to think of myself as having been "busy."

One weekend I was visiting my parents in Morristown, New Jersey, and had taken a new book to show them. I stayed overnight, and when I came down in the morning, I found my parents at the kitchen table. They had obviously been talking about me.

"What is it that you do again?" Mama asked. She had the book on the table in front of her.

"I write stories for children," I said.

"You wrote stories when you were a boy," my father said, emphasizing *boy*. "You're a man, now."

"How do you go about doing it?" Mama asked, interposing herself between me and Dad.

I explained how I would think of an idea, would make an outline of the story, and then type it up and do whatever revisions were necessary. I tried to make the process sound as impressive as I could. I could see in their body language that my father wasn't convinced and that Mama was as pleased as she could be. Later in the day I heard her proudly explaining to a friend on the phone that her son "types stories for a living." I was very pleased.

But my dad, in a way, was right. I had returned to that period of innocence in my life, that period of exploration of the human condition. And I was loving it.

Writing has let me into a world in which I am respected, where the skills I have are respected for themselves. I am in a world of book lovers and people eager to rise to the music of language and ideas. All in all it has been a great journey and not at all shabby for a bad boy.

About the Author

Walter Dean Myers is an award-winning writer of fiction, nonfiction, and poetry for young people. His book *Monster* was the first recipient of the Michael L. Printz Award, as well as a National Book Award Finalist, a Coretta Scott King Honor Book, and a *Boston Globe–Horn Book* Honor Book. His many titles include *Handbook for Boys*; *Crystal*; the Caldecott Honor Book *Harlem*, illustrated by Christopher Myers; and the Newbery Honor Books *Scorpions* and *Somewhere in the Darkness*. He has received the Margaret A. Edwards Award for his contribution to young adult literature and is a five-time winner of the Coretta Scott King Award. Walter Dean Myers lives in Jersey City, New Jersey, with his family.